PRINCETON THEOLOGICAL MONOGRAPH SERIES

Dikran Y. Hadidian

General Editor

9

A LITTLE BOOK OF CHRISTIAN
QUESTIONS AND RESPONSES

A LITTLE BOOK OF CHRISTIAN QUESTIONS AND RESPONSES

In which the principal headings of the Christian Religion are briefly set forth

By

Theodore Beza

Translated by

Kirk M. Summers

PICKWICK PUBLICATIONS
Allison Park, Pennsylvania

Copyright © 1986 by **Pickwick Publications**
4137 Timberlane Drive, Allison Park, PA 15101

Library of Congress Cataloging-in-Publication Data

Bèze, Théodore de, 1519-1605.
  A little book of Christian questions and
responses in which the principal headings of
the Christian religion are briefly set forth.

  (Princeton theological monograph series; 9)
  Translation of: Quaestionum et responsionum
Christianarum libellus.
  1. Theology—Miscellanea. I. Title.
II. Series.
BR96.B4913 1986 238 86-25583
ISBN 0-915138-91-3

TABLE OF CONTENTS

THEODORE BEZA

Theodore Beza stands as one of the greatest paradoxes of the Reformation period. Although few now even know his name, his impact upon his day and age was profound, and the effects of his work are still observable today in reformed Protestantism. His statue stands in Geneva among the four most prominent men of the Swiss Reformation - the others being Calvin, Knox, and Farel. And not without good reason. Theodore Beza was probably the most unusual and colorful of the Sixteenth Century reformers, and he served many functions in his efforts to promote the cause of the Reformation. The accomplishments of his life include the writing of over 75 political, polemical, and theological tracts of wide scholarship and influence. The Huguenots in France, led by Admiral Coligny and Jeanne d'Albret, considered Beza as their key counselor in times of war and peace. It was Beza that led the reformed churches in France through dispute over doctrine with the Catholic Church, representing them at both the Colloquy of Poissy (1561) and New Rochelle (1571). When Calvin needed a rector for the newly established Academy of Geneva in 1559, he turned to Beza as a man of unmatched learning and administrative ability. At Calvin's death Beza was designated by the company of Geneva to assume the load which Calvin had borne. In that position of leadership Beza was able to make Geneva central to the reformed movement.

Theodore Beza was a complex man. Some have tried to categorize him as simply a humanist after the manner of Petrarch, Salutati, Erasmus, and so on. Others, with reasonable foundation, tend to categorize Beza among those who sought to revitalize the scholastic method. In addition, Beza's role as Protestant theologian cannot be denied, nor should his roles as statesman and educator be ignored. Alone, however, none of these categories serve appropriately as a label for Beza, unless one realizes that he is the embodiment of a number of traditions. He is classical humanist, logician, statesman, educator, and theologian all at the same time.

Beza considered his humanistic talents as a vehicle through which he could convey his message. He refused to abandon the techniques and knowledge he had obtained under his childhood instructor Melchior Wolmar. Nevertheless, while early in his life he had sought worldly honors, he soon began to work for the furtherance of the kingdom of God through his gifts. Beza began to view his humanistic education as a vehicle for theological rhetoric, that through the authority and methodology of the ancient authors he could add a greater validity to his positions. Therefore,

Beza increasingly became scholastic in his approach to writing.

It has been alleged that Beza was himself *Calvino Calvinior*, more Calvin than Calvin. And it is true, in certain points of theology Beza went further than Calvin did. For example, it was Beza, not Calvin, who proposed the presbyterian government as the only valid form of church government. Most recent scholarship agrees that the apparent tensions between the theology of Beza and the theology of Calvin were due to changing times. Beza wrote in an era of enlarged controversial discussion on various aspects of theology. With increased controversy comes increased verbiage. In other words, the times in which Beza lived demanded more preciseness of speech and more exactness in details. They required of Beza more careful attention to definitions and distinctions, and thus a scholastic type of approach to theology. In this regard Beza has rendered a great service towards the search for orthodoxy in Protestantism.

QUESTIONS AND RESPONSES

The *Quaestionum et responsionum Christianarum libellus* certainly stands as the crowning achievement of Beza's career. It demonstrates a mature theologian dealing candidly with some complex and vital issues concerning man's relation to God. I suppose if it were possible to place major headings upon this work, they would have to be as follows: The Nature of God, Salvation, Sanctification, and The Eternal Decrees of God. Not everything, however, can be forced under these four major headings.

The work itself consists of 158 pages of Latin in the form of unlabeled *Questions and Responses*. The questioner is unidentified, and the responses are given by Beza himself. Although the format of the work is somewhat similar to a catechism, the content of the discussions far exceeds the normal student's capacity to comprehend and memorize. The style of the work could more closely be linked to the scholastic writers of the late Middle Ages and early Renaissance period.

The *Quaestionum et responsionum Christianarum libellus,* as with most of Beza's works, has been sorely neglected in modern times. Having been first published in 1570, the work was subsequently translated into a few European languages, and even republished in Latin several times. However, no edition in any language was seen after the year 1600 until this present one.

That the works of Beza are absent from the *Corpus Reformatorum,* and that there exists no *opera omnia* is somewhat puzzling. Some have seen Beza as merely a duplicator of the work of Calvin. Others have viewed Beza as a scholastic who altered the purely Biblical theology of Calvin and spawned a more rigid, hyper-Calvinism.

Regardless of one's views, there are many reasons why we should be interested in the writings of Beza. The reader will quickly realize that Beza offers some fresh, new approaches to various questions of theology, all of which are too numerous to list here. But more than that, if we are to understand the directions Calvinism took after the death of Calvin in 1564, we must look to Beza as the one to whom the reins were given. It was Beza who transmitted the tradition to us. The influence of his work can be traced through the sources such as the *Westminster Confession of Faith,* Turretin, Dabney, Heppe, and Berkhof.

Many of the same situations that existed in Beza's day continue to persist in our own. Thus, the need for polemics and reason in defending one's position still exists. And in that regard, we are greatly indebted to Beza.

Beza is truly a link between the purely Biblical approach of John Calvin and the more systematic approach of his predecessors. Too much, however, is made of the tension between what is viewed as the teaching of Calvin and the teaching of the Calvinists. The theology of the Calvinists is basically the same as that of Calvin, but the methodology of modern day systematic theologians is more in line with Beza. Therefore, those in the Calvinist tradition must consider both Calvin and also Calvin's successor, Theodore Beza, as the human founders of what we call the reformed faith.

September, 1986   *Kirk M. Summers*
                                           University of Nebraska
                                           Lincoln, Nebraska

QUESTIONS AND RESPONSES

Q1 **Who placed us in this world?**
A1 God, according to His singular goodness.[1]

Q2 **For what purpose?**
A2 So that we might worship Him, and so that He might be glorified by granting us eternal life.

Q3 **How do we properly worship and glorify Him, thereby acquiring eternal life?**

Rom. 1:21 **A3** By knowing and acknowledging Him according
John 17:3 to how He reveals Himself to us in His own Word.

Q4 **What do you call "the Word of God?"**
A4 That which the Prophets and Apostles recorded
Eph. 2:20 in writings, having received it from the Spirit of God, which book we call the Old and New Testaments.

Q5 **Who, then, is the author of those books?**
Rom. 10:8 **A5** God Himself, however, the Prophets and Apos-
2 Tim. 3:16 tles were His transcribers or amanuenses.
2 Peter 1:20

Q6 **Whence do you know this?**
A6 From the very things which are discussed in
Acts 2:11 those Scriptures: the majesty of God shining
1 Cor. 17-24 forth brightly in that simplicity of speech; the
Luke 21:15 celestial purity and great holiness conspicuous
Acts 6:10 everywhere; the most sure firmness of the
John 5:30 principles on which that doctrine rests; a com-
Acts 17:11 parison of predictions and event. All these things
2 Cor. 4:3 demonstrate more than enough, even to those who most greatly oppose it, that these Scriptures are wholly divine and heavenly, and therefore the most perfect doctrine of truth. The very succession of history also accedes to it, as well as the testimony passed down through the hands
John 6:45 of pious men. Why I know these things so, as
Acts 13:48 I fully assent to those things which some men
Phil. 1:29 are accustomed to spurn and ridicule, and others
Acts 16:14 embrace, yet so that what they profess to believe, they do not understand at all, I owe entirely to the Holy Spirit, who opened my heart that I

might perceive these hidden things in my ears and in my mind.[2]

Q7 **Is that which we must believe in order to be saved included in those Scriptures?**

2 Tim. 3:17

A7 Altogether.

Q8 **What then do the Prophetic and Apostolic Scriptures teach us principally must be believed about God Himself?**

Deut. 6:4
Mt. 28:19
A8 That there is one essence of God, and three persons: Father, Son, and Holy Spirit.[3]

Q9 **What do you mean by "essence?"**
A9 Essence is that nature common to the three persons.

Q10 **What do you mean by "persons?"**
A10 Those who subsist in this very nature.

Q11 **Therefore, are these three persons Gods, just as there are as many men as there are persons endowed with a human nature?[4]**

A11 Not at all, for these three distinct persons are one and the same God.

Q12 **How can this be so?**
A12 Since the essence of God is very simple,[5] infinite and indivisible, therefore these three persons are not separated from one another, but are merely distinct, so that the Father is not the Son or the Holy Spirit, but the Father only; nor is the Son the Father or the Spirit, but only the Son; nor is the Holy Spirit the Father or the Son, but the Holy Spirit only; and these three distinct persons are one and the same perfect God, coeternals, coessentials, and coequals, although in order (but not by rank) the Father is first, being from no one: second there is the Son who is from the Father: third there is the Holy Spirit who is from the Father and the Son. Both are indescribably in eternal communication with the whole essence of God: the Son begotten, and the Spirit proceeding.

Q13 **Inexplicable, I see, is the depth of this mystery.**

A13 It is entirely, if by human reason one should try to comprehend it. But it attests to be so in the expressed Word of God. Therefore, one must believe and adore this mystery that God revealed. Moreover, that which is hidden from us and which we cannot conceive must not be speculated upon.

Q14 **But does this knowledge concerning the essence of God suffice to salvation?**

Rom. 8:15-17
Gal. 4:6,7
John 1:16-17

A14 No, not all. For besides the many other things whereby to a degree the nature of God is depicted to us, first we must know the manner in which He is disposed towards us, lest we make Him like created things.

Q15 **So that you may know this, what in God should you chiefly consider?**

Exo. 20:5,6 **A15** His perfect justice, and perfect mercy.

Exo. 34:6,7

Q16 **What do you mean by "justice" and "mercy?"**

A16 They are not in God, as qualities,[6] but through the justice of God, we know to so great an extent is the nature of God perfect, that He especially hates and most severely will punish all injustice. By the term "perfect mercy" we mean that whatever is bestowed upon us comes entirely from His free grace, especially the gift of eternal life.

Q17 **Yet, these things seem to contradict. For how can He be the most severe punisher of them whom He condones by His free grace?**

A17 The Father has revealed to us that these things agree perfectly in His Son, who paid the penalty for our sins completely, and was freely given to us by the Father.

Q18 **Did not the Father and Holy Spirit undergo death for us?**

John 1:14;
16:13; 17:3
Rom. 8:14

A18 Certainly neither the Father nor the Holy Spirit died for us, but only the Son whom the Father sent, and whom the Holy Spirit instructs and seals in us.

1 John 4:13 **Q19** **Is not the Son a true God by nature, as are the Father and Holy Spirit, and likewise immortal?**

Matt. 1:21 **A19** Yes, for He could not be our Saviour unless He
Mark 2:7 was God.

Q20 **How, then, was He able to die?**

Gal. 4:45 **A20** He became a man so that He, who according to
Heb. 2:9,14,15 His divinity is eternal life itself, might die in the flesh.

Q21 **Yet the Son is God unchangeable. How, then, did He become a man?**

A21 Not by the mixing of natures or properties, or by
John 1:14 any metamorphosis of God into man, or man
Heb. 2:16 into God, is this done, but by the close and
1 John 1:7 personal union of the God Son with the assumed nature of man, so that the Son of God remains one person, truly God and truly man, Jesus Christ.[7]

Q22 **What sort of union is this?**

A22 In the Greek it is said to be a *hypostatic* union, and in the Latin it is said to be a *personal* union.

Q23 **Please explain it to me so that I can understand how it is possible.**

A23 Things are said to be united in nature which come together into one nature, whether it happens apart from any compacting, mixing, or change, just as the three divine persons are one substance; or united by composition alone, as the soul and body, which combine to constitute that which is man; or united by some intervening mixture or change as happens in the changing of elements and mixed things. However, something is said to be mixed personally, or hypostatically, which is so joined that from the union there arises one and the same hypostasis, or person: just as the soul and body are so united to constitute one human nature, so that in one person or one individual they combine.[8] Of such a kind also is the union of the natures in Christ, not joining to form a *tertium quid*,[9] as

Eutychus[10] falsely believed, but joining to form one hypostasis, or person, apart from any confusion of the very natures or essential properties. Moreover, I mean a union of natures, not hypostases, for one person should not be thought of as derived from two persons, since there is in Christ one substance, that of the Word, in which subsists the other assumed nature, the human nature. For a person did not assume a person, but the divine nature in the person of the One Son (that is, insofar as the Son, not the Father and the Holy Spirit, subsist in it) assumed a human nature devoid from any distinct personality (as I would say). In sum then, just as in God there are three persons joined into one and the same nature, so in Christ there are two natures joined into one hypostasis of the Son, so that the three persons are not three Gods, but one God, according to a most simple triune of persons into one and the same united nature. Nor are there two Christs, but one Christ; not two perfect persons, but two natures; not joined to constitute a third nature, but united into the one person of the Son, in which both natures are sustained.

Q24 **Likewise, I do not understand this mystery.**

A24 Then again adore what you cannot grasp. For all of Scripture proclaims it to be most true; and unless it is so, we have no *Jesus*, which means "Savior," or *Christ*, which means, "one anointed as our highest and eternal King, Prophet, and Priest."

Q25 **But was God not able to save man by another method less removed from our senses?**

A25 Certainly He was able, but this method was greatly suited for declaring, not only His justice, but also His mercy.

Q26 **How so?**

A26 Because if He saved us apart from full satisfac-

Heb. 2:14-17
Rom. 8:3

2 Cor. 5:19

Rom 5:8

tion, or should He fulfill this satisfaction from another nature than that of the guilty party, it would seem to be unmindful of His own justice; therefore, it is proper that our Saviour became a man. But if He were only a man, He would not be able to exhaust the wrath of God, and thus would not be able to extricate Himself or save us. Therefore, it was necessary for the assumed flesh to be sustained by His divine nature and that perfect union. Further, in regards to mercy, is there able to be set forth any more certain, clear, even divine testimony to most perfect mercifulness, than that the Father gave His only Son for His own enemies, and that the Son bared His own soul for unrighteous people?

Q27 **It is so. But was not Christ Himself guiltless?**

A27 Certainly. Therefore, He was conceived by the Holy Spirit in the virgin Mary, not only utterly unblemished with any spot, but also endowed with the greatest integrity and purity in the flesh. Otherwise, He Himself would need a saviour, and even His own sacrifice would not satisfy God. No, God would not join Himself to an impure nature.

Matt. 1:20
Rom. 8:3
1 Peter 3:18

Q28 **But is it suitable to God's great justice to punish someone else's sins on an innocent, most holy man?**

A28 Clearly, the Father would seem to be unjust, if He punished the Son as guilty. Therefore, He did not punish Him as if He were guilty, but as one who wished to present Himself of His own accord as a way for the unrighteous. In this manner, God did nothing that was contrary to His justice.

2 Cor. 5:18

Q29 **But why was He condemned before the tribunal of a judge, and afflicted by the suffering of the cross, when He could have died for us in another way?**

A29 So that it might be even more apparent that He became a curse for us, and that all the wrath of the Father against our sins was received in Himself, in order that we might be fully liberated.

Q30 **But death is suitable to the body only. Therefore, it seems that only our bodies are freed by His death. Still, we all die. Thus it appears that He is the saviour of neither the soul nor the body.**

A30 It was proper that a soul also be assumed by Christ together with the body, not only so that He could die (for the first death is a separation of the soul from the body), but also so that, having been made a complete man, He could liberate the whole and complete man.[11]

Q31 **Therefore, you mean that He endured the sufferings with which our souls are afflicted.**

Gal. 3:13

A31 Altogether. For this is probably the chief part of the sufferings of Christ, that besides enduring the greatest tortures of a severe death, He sustained the awful weight of the wrath of God against our sin. Nothing can be more terrible than that. Clearly, with the Godhead inactive in Him through that time, yet so that the assumed human nature did not expire, even under this weight which would have been intolerable to the very angels, nevertheless He felt very sharply the whole wrath of God unspeakably inflamed against all the sins of all the elect. He experienced it and endured it to the end, until the satisfaction was full. Therefore, during the time He hung on the cross, He abided in the middle of the tortures of Hell,[12] so that He could liberate us fully from both deaths.

Q32 **But then, if He came to liberate us from death, why did He Himself die?**

Heb. 2:14
Isa. 53:8
Hos. 13:14

A32 Because otherwise the great justice of God, which needed to be satisfied, would not be manifest in our redemption. And more glorious still on that account is the victory of Christ, because by dying He conquered death.

Q33 **Why, then, do the elect still die, if death was conquered for them by Christ?**

A33 Because Christ did not come to restore us into the station of this world which was lost in Adam, but in order to transfer us into a far better immortality; but that is not able to happen unless we migrate from this world. Therefore, although this separation of body and spirit, which is called the first death, arises from sin, whose remnants are even in the most holy men, nevertheless, if you consider the counsel and plan of God, death is not imposed upon the elect by God as judge, but was sent by a most kind Father calling His own nearer to Himself. Thus envisioned, it not only does not frighten believers, it actually renews and refreshes them.

Rom. 5:15

1 Cor. 15:35

Q34 **Why, then, does his power not avail itself against death immediately?**

A34 On the contrary, it did reveal itself immediately, since His body had experienced no corruption. Nevertheless, He willed that He be placed in the tomb for an interval, both so that His death being true, even having been confirmed by the seals of His enemies, might prove His subsequent resurrection, and also that He might as victor pursue Death into the innermost part of his own cave; and so He sprinkles our tombs with the vivific odor of His own death.

Matt. 28

Acts 2:24

Rom. 6:4

Q35 **Then is the resurrection a witness that He willingly approached death, that He might prepare immortality for us?**

A35 Yes it is, since by His own power He arose never to die again, so that we might be restored in Him to eternal life.

Rom. 6:10

1 Cor. 15:3ff

Q36 **However, why did He ascend into the heavens, rather than abide with us?**

A36 With His body He did indeed depart from us among whom He was, above all the heavens where formerly He had no body. He did this,

Eph. 4:8-10

1 Cor. 15-20 not only so that, while triumphing over His captive enemies, He might begin the possession of the heavenly kingdom as the first one who rose from the dead, but also so that He might instruct *John 14:2* us to strive for that location where He has prepared a place for us. Meanwhile, He is very present by His own Spirit, governing the Church as the head over the members joined to it.

Col. 3:1

Q37 **Therefore, He changed locations, so that He departed to where there is no place.**

A37 Yes, He changed His location, as history testifies, *Matt. 28:20* and as the fact that He has a body, albeit glorified, demands. But He changed locations according to that nature which is physically restricted, yet not so that He might desert us (for He is still present with us with His full power, since He is truly God, and Christ is one person, both God and man at the same time), but so that He might teach us to withdraw from the earth to seek heavenly things. Moreover, that you say there is no place where He ascended is an empty description. Let it suffice, that the Godhead alone is infinite; all other things, whether in heaven, or above the heavens, or in the earth, or below it (and even though His body is glorified, it is still truly a human body), are by its nature finite and physically limited. How they are contained in that eternal glory will be clearer to us when we also go there.

Q38 **In this way you appear to divide Christ, or to make two Christs, one here, the other there.**

A38 I do not divide Christ, but I remove the confusion of the natures, when I say that He is departed according to His flesh. Yet that which is according to His deity is present, and if He is considered as a whole thing, that is, as a whole person, both God and man are present.[13]

Q39 **What does His sitting at the right hand of the Father show?**

A39 That He is elevated into the high position of

glory which is above every name, with the reality of his flesh not laid aside, but all infirmity; with the flesh already fully glorified by the deity dwelling in it, yet not absorbed into His essence nor into His essential properties; and with Him governing and administrating with full justice all things in heaven and on earth (except Him who subjects all things to Him).

Phil. 2:9
Col. 2:9
Matt. 28:18
Heb. 2:8,9
1 Cor. 15:17

Q40 **What do you mean by "essential properties?"**

A40 That which, when removed, by necessity causes the thing to be no longer what it was. Thus, for example, the body, with quantity removed, necessarily ceases to be a body.

Luke 24:39

Q41 **And yet God is omnipotent.**

A41 Who denies this?

Q42 **Therefore, He is able to cause one and the same body to be in many places at the same time, or somewhere to be as in a place and not as in a place at the same time, but by some incomprehensible manner.**

A42 That God is able to make it happen so that something that is, is not anymore, just as He made it happen so that something which was not, is, no one, unless He is insane, doubts, since it is so obvious that He is able to change the forms and qualities of things at will. But to make it happen so that something is and is not at the same time, or is such and is not such at the same time, God is not able to do, because He is not able to lie. Indeed, to not be able to lie is not a weakness, but is a sign of invariable strength.

Q43 **You conclude, then, that Christ, touching His humanity, is now away from us.**

A43 Altogether, and, indeed, by as much space as that which is above the heavens (where that flesh is exalted) is away from the earth (where we are).

Col. 3:1

Q44 **Still, He said that He was presently in heaven, even while speaking to Nicodemus on the earth.**

John 3:13

A44 That, as well as other things of this type, are understood in reference to the communication of idioms.

Q45 **What are "idioms?"**
A45 That which the dialectics call proper to the fourth mode:[14] of which manner is (for example) infinity in the divine nature, and quantity in all things created, especially, bodily things.

Q46 **Then this communication is false, since an idiom of this type ceases to be an idiom, as soon as it becomes common.**
A46 This latter point I simply concede, but not the first one.

Q47 **But these two things seem to cohere absolutely.**
A47 Then understand it in this way: there remains of each nature in Christ, Godhead and manhood, their own essential properties, so as we have said, they are incommunicable; because unless we say this, infinite absurdities and certainly impieties follow. For the Godhead would be transformed into the manhood by those properties of the human nature which it receives into itself, and contrawise, the humanity, by the communication of the properties of the Godhead, would become a certain fictitious Godhead, so that Christ could not be said to be true God or true man, and likewise He would not be a saviour for us. Therefore, there is neither any communication of natures or essential properties, and how false and impious are those declarations, 'The flesh is Godhead, the Godhead is flesh.'' Likewise are these statements false and impious, "The flesh of Christ is everywhere," or, "Christ is ubiquitous according to the flesh," or, "Christ is not ubiquitous according to His Godhead." And these, therefore, are most false, "The Godhead was crucified," or, "The Godhead died; the flesh of Christ is infinite." However, although these natures might be unique with their own essential, incommunicable

properties, as I have said, nevertheless, they are united to so great an extent, that they are as one and the same substance, or constitute one person. Therefore, how false are these declarations, "The Godhead is flesh and the flesh is Godhead," yet, how true and orthodox are these, "God (that is, the Word) is a man, and a man is God," on account of the unity of person, arising not from the communication of natures, which we have said there is no such thing (unless you take communication for union, which is wholly improper), but from the union of natures. For God is not a man inasmuch as He is God (which nevertheless would follow if the natures of the essences themselves were communicable). But in another respect He is a man, inasmuch as He united a man to Himself. Nor is a man God, inasmuch as He is a man. But in another respect man is God, that is, inasmuch as He is united to God. What truly we have said concerning the natures themselves, also must be said concerning the essential and equally incommunicable properties. Therefore, most true are these declarations by a like manner of explanation: God (that is, the Word), was conceived, born, suffered, was crucified, died, buried, and He arose, inasmuch as He clearly united man to Himself, but not inasmuch as He is God. And these things of like manner are most true: a man is the Son of God, infinite, invisible, filling all things: not in and of itself, that is, inasmuch as He is man, nor by any communication of properties, but inasmuch as He is assumed into one person by the Son of God.

Q48 **But these formulas of speaking seem hard and very strange.**

A48 On the contrary, if you would remove your prejudiced opinion, it is very useful for showing the union of the natures, which is so great, that what is not able to be said concerning the abstract, namely the Godhead or the humanity, nevertheless is attributed to the concrete, of one or the other, namely to the God or to the man.[15] Because clearly from the two natures is not made one nature, but one person. Therefore, we place a certain union in the natures, but not a unity, but merely a unity of person. From whence it happens that this whole person is signified, not only by the very name of the whole person, namely Jesus, which includes both the natures united together, but also by the word of either nature (yet considered concretely, not abstractly), namely God or man. The same is true in regard to the word *Christ*, that is to say "anointed." Although it refers properly to the human nature only (for the Godhead is not anointed, but anoints), nevertheless it means the whole person. Moreover, it is very common in all languages to speak concerning persons in a similar manner, to show the unity of the parties from which the unity of the person is constituted. Thus, this way of speaking is very proper: "Peter is an Apostle," certainly agreeing with the whole person and his single parts, namely, the spirit and body of Peter. Truly this: "Peter is the son of Jonas," agrees with him as a certain whole together, and is considered as a whole thing, that is to say, considered according to the unity of the person, and not with his single parts, except only in respect to one part, namely, the body - unless perhaps you think that the spirit is also transferred.[16] It is a similar form of speaking when we call someone mortal or intelligent, which agrees to the whole person as a whole according to the unity of person, nevertheless only in respect to one or the other part. Yes, so great is the power of this personal union, that even after the dissolving of it, one still might speak in similar formulas, like if you should say, "Peter lies in Rome (we will assume it to be so)." It would be a true declaration, yet only in respect to the body, although you call it by the name Peter, that is, the whole person.

Q49 **Why, then, do you call it the communication of idioms, if there is no real communication of natures and essential properties.**

A49 We do not call the communication of properties the personal union itself, or the form of this union, but the proclamation, as the dialectics say, which is on account of the personal union of the two natures, in which an essential property or operation that agrees to one nature is attributed to the person concretely, and not abstractly. Moreover, since this proclamation is true, it is necessary that it be based on truth, nevertheless, in the same way, namely, in respect to the whole person considered concretely.

Q50 **Again, therefore, you conclude that Christ, touching His flesh, truly and really has migrated from the earth above all the heavens, and thus is now absent from us who are in the earth.**

A50 Yes, although I believe that Christ as man is most present with us, but in another regard, that is, inasmuch as this same man is also God. Yes, if you are willing, I will even concede that the humanity of Christ is also present, but in another regard, that is, not in and of itself in its essence, but inasmuch as it is joined to the omnipresent Word by hypostatic union. Therefore, it is indeed present in the Table itself.

Q51 **What advantage is Christ for us now, if we are deserted by Him?**

A51 Indeed, He never deserted us, since now, according to His own glorified flesh, He administers all things in heaven and on earth, with the name which is above every name received from the Father. Moreover, relying on this His power, He quickens His Church in this world by His

Matt. 28:18
John 17:2
Matt. 28:20
John 15:4
Gal. 2:20

Eph. 1:11 mysterious and unspeakable power, and cherishes, and governs it, and at the same time reigns in the midst of all His enemies. Moreover, in heaven He intercedes all the while before the Father, until the ultimate enemy, clearly death, is utterly destroyed.

Q52 **Please tell me what kind of intercession is this?**

A52 He intercedes first by pacifying the Father for us with the perpetual vigor of His own innocence and obedience; then, He also intercedes because we are not able to rightly address the Father except in His name, thus as always He intervenes between us and the Father as mediator, so that whatever we offer to the Father may be pleasing. Moreover, that some dream concerning the supplication of Christ and His humbling at the knee of the Father is an empty comment of those men who do not know to distinguish the infirm Christ from the glorified Christ, nor heavenly things from earthly things.

Q53 **What, then, do you think about those who stubbornly hold that Christ is not a mediator according to both natures?**

A53 I consider them to be an instrument of the Devil, united to impede the work of the Lord, which experience itself has confirmed.

Q54 **Yet to be a mean[17] implies there is an inferior place to a higher, and it is for the lesser person to be a mediator to the greater. Hence I gather that they seem to be Arians who hold the opinion that Christ, according to His Deity, is also mean and mediator.**

A54 I would marvel that any men would be able to be found in so great a light of the Gospel, who allow themselves to be ensnared by such simple deceptions, unless the reality of it showed that they never followed the Gospel of God with a right zeal. I speak concerning the inflexible type and those who are self-condemned by their own actions.

Q55 **But this is not an answer.**

A55 The indignity of the thing compelled me to erupt into these words, since I see that so many have deserted for small or no occasion, initially to Arianism, then later to Tritheism, and finally to the unholy dotings of Samosetane. Come then, let us inquire concerning each one in order.

Q56 **Therefore, do you think a *mean* is the same as a *mediator*?**

A56 Altogether. For mean speaks of the very quality of a person, so that the thing between two extremes is considered a mean. But a mediator denotes a go-between or conciliator, which two things are so diverse, that one might be a mediator, who nevertheless is not in the middle position, as when we reconcile people to people; and contrawise, someone who is a mean, is not necessarily a mediator.

Q57 **Yet Christ is both mediator and mean.**

A57 I concede that.

Q58 **If He is a mean inasmuch as He is the God Word, or Son, then the Son is inferior to the Father, namely, possessed with some deity that is mean between the highest deity of the Father and the nature of men.**

A58 Then you consider Christ to be a mean according to only one nature, that is, His human nature, or in no manner at all.

Q59 **No, but respond to that which I have stated first.**

A59 Therefore, I respond that whichever of the natures you have in mind, Christ cannot be called a mean, since inasmuch as He is God, the Son is equal to the Father: and inasmuch as He is man, He is equal to the remaining men. Therefore, if He is a mean in this way, it would be necessary for Him to consist of some mean nature, in which He would be neither in the highest degree, God, nor in the lowest, man; which in no manner can be granted.[18]

Q60 **Therefore, if Christ is not a mean in respect to either of His two natures, it follows that He is in no way a mean.**

A60 Not if you consider the natures united, joined together into one and the same person, as you must do, and not by themselves, as those troublers of the church are wont to do. Therefore Christ as one is a mean, since He is in the same way God as He is man, and thus in some sense inferior to the Father, namely, according to the assumed form of the servant. And He is in the same way man as He is God, and thus superior to the angels themselves, and much more eminent above men, but in a certain respect, namely, on account of the assuming form of God. Therefore, He is mean according to both natures joined together in personal union, but not according to either considered alone. For in Christ is indeed one thing and another, but not one person and another.

Q61 **What do you think about the office of the mediator?**

A61 The same as I think concerning the mean. For these things always cohere in Christ, since, just as He is made mean by the union of the natures, so He should be mediator between the Father and men.

Q62 **Therefore, Christ was not a mediator according to either nature considered by itself?**

A62 No, because the Word has not, apart from those things which pertain to the flesh, reconciled men to the Father; nor has the man Himself emerged as the victor, still less has he been our deliverer, except He was man at the same time as He was God. Nevertheless, this is the difference, that the Word used the works of the assumed manhood, not from necessity, but by mere will.

Truly, it behooved the man necessarily to borrow this efficacy from the assuming nature of the God. In this work of mediation, that is, reconciliation, some are works of the whole person, that is, both natures working at the same time, while some are attributed distinctly to the deity, and some distinctly to the humanity. In sum, neither nature by itself has been a mediatorship.

Q63 **But what do we believe concerning the office of intercession. For certainly, He is inferior who intercedes before another.**

A63 This is very false. What prevents an equal from interceding to an equal for another man, or for a superior to an inferior? For it clearly does not follow that the Son is less than the Father, even if He had taken these matters unto Himself voluntarily apart from any assumed flesh. But already we have shown that the things which are written concerning the intercession of Christ must not be accommodated to the rationale convenient to the sovereigns and degrees of this world. Furthermore, how the Word is a mean between the Father and us in respect to the union of natures, and how by reason of His office He is held as mediator between the Father and us, we have already declared.

Q64 **Also, they say that it seems that the Godhead intercedes before itself, if Christ, inasmuch as he is God, is also called intercessor.**

A64 Indeed they say it, but unskillfully. For although in the Son and in the Father and in the Holy Spirit the Godhead is whole and perfect, being indivisible, nevertheless we do not consider this Godhead in persons except relatively. Therefore, I posit, because it is most true, that Christ even in His deity which is united to the human nature makes intercession for us before the Father, and yet it is not so that He makes intercession before Himself, since one is the Father, the other is the

Son, with distinct hypostases, although, if the essence is absolutely considered, the Father and Son are one thing, and one God. For just as in Christ there is one thing and another, but not one person and another, so in God is there one person and another, but not one thing (essence) and another.[19]

Q65 **What do you think about the invocation of angels and dead saints?[20]**

A65 It is wrongful, impious idolatry.

Q66 **Yet the angels and saints can be invoked by those who allow no idols to be fabricated. They also must be distinguished who invoke true and blessed angels, or the spirits of pious and holy men, from those who worship fictitious deities as if they were gods, that is, demons and those who by their own admittance are wicked.**

A66 I confess that, not only are sins unequal, but also that those guilty of the same sin are not always equally guilty. But he who sins more grievously, does not exempt by the number of sinners the one who sins less grievously. Therefore, let us put an end to this entire matter, concerning which we have no dispute. Hands make idols, vain fantasies conceive them. And likewise, those are also idolaters, whose idol lurks like an unformed conception in the womb of their imagination; nor is there any kind of idol more loathsome than that which is gathered into the very inward parts of the mind.

Matt. 11:22
John 19:11

Q67 **But why do you call idolatry that which springs from good reason?**

A67 Away with that reason which, not only is not initiated by the Word of God, but also is openly set against it![21] And yet, I cannot see what good reason is able to be brought forth to confirm so crass an evil.

Q68 **What is this matter, I ask, that you say without substantiation?**

A68   To invoke the absent, to whom you are not able to intimate the thinking of your mind, is a matter of extreme foolishness. And to suppose that the souls of the deceased, either are present everywhere, or that, as they are absent, and do not hear the words, still they understand the thoughts of the mind. I say that both of these are a wicked manifestation of idolatry, if only it is idolatry to transfer to the creature, the thing which is proper only to God. And that they make exceptions, so that God reveals our petitions to the spirits of the deceased, or that they gaze at all things in some kind of special looking glass of the trinity, how easy it is to say! - so easy that it it is best to repudiate it as a foolish and crass comment.[22] But also, concerning the angels, we hear that the Lord uses the service of them to protect his children, and there is no doubt that they discharge their duty as it is mandated to them, and are careful concerning the welfare of the godly. But how is it done in faith, since we do not know when they come or go, or whether they are present or away, nor can we find any word or example of this kind of thing in the sacred scriptures, and even less did the angels allow any external religious adoration? Finally, since there is none comparable either in power or in love towards us with Christ, God and man, sitting at the right hand of the Father, so that he, as the only mediator of God and man, might intercede for us, from whence comes this crowd of subordinate intercessors, except from open distrust in him? But concerning the unfailing love of the saints, which some harp upon, although it is true, nevertheless, it is so absurdly applied to proving the doctrine of praying to the saints, that it is worthy of no refutation.

Q69   **Still, we pray one for another, and we desire the prayers of one another. The apostle Paul himself is an example before us. Therefore, to**

ask for the intercession of someone other than Christ does not detract from the office of the one mediator to whom we do not say, "Pray for us," but, "Have mercy on us."

A69 First, it is certain that those who hold to praying to angels and dead ones, do not hold themselves within these limits, but seek their help in their perils and difficulties, as the most open idolaters of old did seek aid from those deities collected beneath the throne of Juppiter. Then again, for the members of the same body to seek prayers among themselves, so long as we are able to make others aware of our affairs in this life, it is clearly not praying to men, or subordinating Christ, which they do, but rather, it is a praying together with our brethren in the name of the same mediator to the Father, which one-mindedness is a very pleasing sacrifice to God.

Q70 But the Holy Spirit Himself is said to make intercession for us.

Rom. 8:26

A70 Yes, because He teaches you to groan and to pray rightly, even as He is said to shout by the same apostle.

Rom. 8:15

Q71 But when will this intercession end?

A71 Truly never, not even at that time when we shall have appeared with God will we cleave to Him, unless by the intervention of a mean or mediator, and consequently of our head Jesus Christ. His reign and priesthood are eternal by the same reason. Still, this entire method of ruling and governing the Church will cease, after the last enemy is defeated, death, and all the elect are brought up with their head into eternal life. God will be all in all.

Q72 But Paul says this kingdom will be given up to the Father, and that Christ will be subjected to Him.

1 Cor. 15:28

A72 Paul, considering Christ as the true Son of God, but manifest in the flesh and joined with his members, correctly attributes to the Godhead the highest glory, which then will be greatly revealed, when all enemies are defeated. And truly this subjection demonstrates something inferior to this very Godhead (for creatures, even those in Christ, are never equal to the creator), but still, he shows that the greatest blessedness, following that which is proper to the Godhead, rests in this: that God along with our head, inasmuch as He is a man on behalf of his dear and faithful subjects, having accepted us will bless us at last, and will punish the rest as rebels with endless penalties.

Q73 **But the fact that He will come on the last day to judge the quick and the dead, is not without difficulty. For it is evident from many passages of Scripture, and especially from the story or parable of the rich glutton, that the judgement of good and bad men soon follows the departure from this life.**

2 Tim. 4:1

Luke 16:19

Luke 16:22-24

A73 God to a certain degree does execute His judgement (or rather, prejudgement) even then, to such an extent that it must not be doubted that the joy of eternal life is tasted by the souls of the godly, and that the torments of Hell are experienced by the souls of the ungodly. However, the prejudgement has only to do with souls, while their bodies are still sleeping in the dust, for the full declaration and execution of judgement whereby the whole man is made either a possessor of eternal life, or is sent into eternal torture, is delayed until that last day of the resurrection.

Acts 7:60

Phil. 1:23

Matt. 25:33

Q74 **Therefore, you do not understand the dead to be those who will be dead at that time when they will be judged, but those who formerly were dead who at that time will have resurrected. Who, then, do you understand to be the quick ones, as opposed to those dead ones?**

A74 Those whom Christ will find still surviving in

1 Cor. 15:51,52
1 Thess. 4:15

this life at the time of His second, most glorious advent, for whom the change into either state of the future, whether eternal death or everlasting life, will be without death and resurrection, as the apostle teaches.[23]

Q75 **How can they be said to be damned with eternal death, who nevertheless will have risen never to die?**

A75 Because to live in such horrible and indescribable torments both of soul and body, does not deserve the name life, but rather death.

Q76 **But is not the resurrection in general from the kindness of God and in Christ, who is the first fruits of them that rise?**

A76 Just as in the Son the Father created all things, likewise shall the wicked receive life, that is, by the intervention of his power. But the blessing of life is a curse for the wicked, as all other things are. Therefore, the wicked will not rise again by the benefit and virtue of the resurrection of Christ (for this resurrection is knit by an inseparable knot with a blessed life, and so only those who believe and are grafted to Christ become participants of it), by the authority and power of the Son as Judge, who, when He pronounced His sentence of double death and especially of eternal death against the human race, did even then damn men (except those whom He would save from death) with the penalty of resurrection. For how is the penalty of the wicked eternal (as if it is always future) if their bodies forever stay in the dust, destitute of all their senses?

1 Cor. 15:22

Gen. 2:17
Gen. 3:19

Q77 **Yet, since the body does not move in and of itself, but is only an instrument of the soul, it seems only right that the whole penalty of the sinner or glory of the just should fall on men's souls.**

A77 The whole of Scripture contradicts that as often

1 Cor. 15:35   as it mentions the resurrection, which does not avail itself in souls alone. Also, since the body does not sin by itself, but rather the whole man sins, it is right that the whole man be punished. Moreover, Christ would not be a complete *1 Thess. 5:23*   redeemer, if He would desert the bodies of His *Heb. 2:14*   own in a rotten state, neither would He have had need of assuming a body, if He came only to liberate our souls.

Q78 **But what manner will that eternal life and everlasting death be?**

A78 Those who investigate these things do sin in vain, not only because the curiosity which drives us to seek out the things which the Lord has hidden from us must be condemned, but also because it is of extreme madness to want to comprehend that which you are not capable of comprehending. Truly, if now we were able to grasp that blessedness, already we would in a measure be possessors of it, since the intellect at least enjoys the thing understood to the degree that it understands it. Nor otherwise should we think concerning the eternal penalties, of which we see that even a faint apprehension now and then drives men to despair and horrible actions. Therefore, that men do not yet fully understand the horror of that eternal fire, must be attributed to the patience of God delaying His wrath. Thus we should instead seek by what road we might reach the point, so that we might hold the way of life. And let us acquiesce in those things which the Lord has revealed to us in His word concerning these matters, that the future happiness of the godly and the unhappiness of the ungodly will be so great that the manner and measure of neither is able to be comprehended.

Q79 **Then what is the way to eternal life?**

A79 Christ Himself, as He Himself testified. There is *John 10:7-9*   no other road which leads to life.

Q80 But He does not quicken all men.

A80 I agree, He does not quicken any but those who walk into this way. Moreover, to walk into this way is to join oneself to Christ by believing, and also, to a certain extent, to incorporate oneself to Him.

Q81 What is faith?

Rom. 8:38

A81 The faith whereby the sons of light are distinguished from the sons of darkness, is not simply that recognition of the facts common among the demons themselves, whereby it happens that one acknowledges those things to be true which are contained in the writings of the prophets and apostles. Rather, it is a firm assent of one's mind accompanying that recognition of the facts, whereby it happens that each man applies particularly to himself the promise of eternal life in Christ Jesus, just as if he already were actually a possessor of it.[24]

Q82 Does nature furnish us with this faith, or does grace, or perhaps partly both?

A82 It is given by the mere grace of God who regenerates.

Q83 Is there not a recognition of God and common insight present in man although his nature is corrupt?

Matt. 16:17
John 1:15-19
1 Cor. 2:9-14

Col. 2:2
1 Thess. 1:5

A83 Yes, they are in man, but they are as the rubbish of a very magnificent building. Again I say this, that this faith is not grounded in natural insight.[25] Those things must be included which God has formerly and particularly revealed to the world through the prophets and apostles, concerning which flesh and blood would never have been able to think. Lastly, this also must be noted in which is grounded the special difference of faith: everyone must apply peculiarly to himself the promise of eternal life in Christ by believing, which testimony the scripture calls the assurance of understanding.

Q84 Let us digress a little, please, and let us discuss the corruption of man. First, I ask what you consider to be corrupt in man, then what manner of corruption is it? Lastly, what do you consider to be the remedy against it?

John 3:6
Eph. 2:5

A84 To the first question I respond that the whole man is corrupt, to such a degree that Paul said we are dead in our trespasses. Every aspect of man must be understood in this passage.

Q85 Does this corruption touch his very essence?

A85 Yes, it touches that which pertains to the body, which thus has become mortal. We must think otherwise concerning the soul.

Q86 What shall we think concerning the corruption of the soul?

A86 That it is corrupt in qualities which, for the sake of instructing I now make two, namely, reason and will.

Q87 Then do you include these qualities in the soul?

A87 Yes, but consistent with a spiritual and single nature. Otherwise, if a soul or spirit is nothing but an essence, come, let us make as many secondary gods as there are human souls. But so that we might all at once avoid the many obscure questions of the scholastics, know that I place only one soul in man, since I do not read that there are many conditions in him, and I judge it an absurdity that one body is animated by many souls. Again, through the qualities of the soul I know two things: first, the faculties grounded in the soul itself, which I say must no less be distinguished from the substance of the soul (yet by a distinction which is consistent with a spiritual nature) than the power of drawing iron is distinguished from the substance of a magnet; second, the wholeness or rightness, or, as Moses termed it, the goodness of these faculties which I say is twofold.

Q88 But since the fall of man is not sufficiently able to be deeply understood or described, they who say original sin rests only in accidents or qualities, seem to consider it a superficial evil, and one that adheres as if only to the skin.

A88 These are the thoughts of inept men, and likewise did Satan once deceive certain men, who wished to bend Christian dogmas to the norm of their own foolish reason. By those qualities we do not mean extraneous and chance accidents,[26] but things which adhere to the nature itself, and yet they may be severed from the very essence and material in which they are, not in reality, but by reason and thought.

Q89 Therefore, you say in sum, that the qualities of the soul are corrupt, but not the essence.

A89 I say so, and I say that the contrary dogma is a certain and open road to Epicureanism, that is, to hold to the mortality of the soul. For should we posit the slightest corruption of the essence itself, it is necessary to confess that it is liable to perishing. Again, if the corruption is of the whole soul, it is necessary that the whole soul immediately perish. But if the corruption is in parts, how can there be a division of parts in a simple essence, such as the soul is? Thus, one has to be notably insane to hold such an absurd and ungodly dogma, and no less blind are they who lend an ear to them.

Q90 Let us leave this matter, the delight of those on whom God will execute his just judgements. Now, come, tell me what is this corruption?

A90 Neither will nor intelligence is removed, as I have already said, because it would be necessary for the soul to then perish, or for the soul to cease existing, if these things were removed. But both of these faculties are so injured, that whereas the eye of understanding ought to have been very clear (even as it was before the Fall), especially in divine things and those things

Rom. 1:20

which pertain to a right conscience; partly it sees nothing at all, not even with the light of the Creator Himself set before it, as it is seen in the chief points of the true religion, which man's reason not only loathes, but also fights as absurd and false for all men; partly, if it should see, it sees very dimly to the extent that those small traces of light (some measure of which is innate in every soul; some who have been intent on considering sublime things have perceived more things), having been left in man to the end so that man is without excuse, they will leave a man in the vestibule of truth, not to mention that, with the torch going before, he might come all the way to the very sanctuary of the truth. And further, in regard to equity that can be observed between men, although the sharpness of the human mind is somewhat less dull in this, God so moderates His just judgement, so that the society of the human race from which he collects His church, might more easily be preserved.[27] Otherwise, soon that society would have been annihilated, in accordance as the fall of man merits, if all discrimination of right and wrong, virtue and vice had been removed from the minds of men. The repugnancies, not only in the opinions of the vulgar, where there are as many opinions as there are heads, but also in the judgements of the most wise philosophers and lawyers, in which making them agree many recently have wearied themselves in vain, prove that still the blindness of men is very great, both in discussing general things, but especially in discussing hypothetical things. Now I descend to the other faculty of the mind,[28] which is the seat of the affections. Although it ought to be ruled by reason as by one that handles reins, how often does it snatch him away headlong? It is no marvel, then, when it sometimes snatches away even the soul itself. I omit the unruliness of all the natural affections, which evil reason,

Rom. 7:18,19

Rom. 7:8ff fighting against it, sees and condemns, but only the law of God utterly detects it. But to that darkness whereby the faculty of reason and will is overcast, still another worse evil is added, that reason feeds upon untruth, and wrestles willfully against the wisdom of God, even when convicted; and that the will is carried willfully to vice even against the reprehensions of reason, and is not able to flee or strive after anything rightly, since it has been completely enslaved to sin.

Q91 Are we but logs then?[29]
A91 Not at all. For when I say that the reason and will of man are blind and perverse, I do not strip man of the faculty of reasoning or willing.

Q92 Therefore, you take away free will.
A92 If by *free* you mean *spontaneous*, I am far from doing that; to the contrary, I would say that the whole soul is carried to evil willingly and spontaneously.[30] But if by *free* you mean that it has any ableness of itself to either, that is, to even

Rom. 3:10 be inclined to good, I deny this completely, relying on the nearly infinite testimonies of all of Scripture, and taught by perpetual experience. For you are not able to bring forth anyone among the number of men (except among the saints) who truly knows good, much less one who desires it.

Q93 What do you do, then, with the philosophical virtues?
A93 First, I say that many of the true virtues did not come into the mind of philosophers who were not Christians; also, that those virtues which they did know were not described fully enough by them; finally, that no man has ever been found gifted with philosophical virtues in any age apart from regeneration.

Q94 But certainly philosophical virtues are not sins.
John 3:3-5 **A94** Yes, they are sins, if sin is unlawfulness, that

is, anything even slightly removed from the law of God.

Q95 **But with the necessity of sinning posited (for it is necessary to posit it if consultation and choice are removed), you seem thereby to remove sin.**

A95 This consequence is false in many ways. For necessity does not excuse one from fault, if one willingly has thrown himself into the confines of it. And as for this necessity of which I now speak, it is not from nature, but from the voluntary fall of man. Second, I take away neither deliberation nor choice, but I do say that the unregenerate man is not able not to deliberate, and not able not to choose evilly, on account of the utterly corrupt faculty of reasoning and willing.

Q96 **But it seems ridiculous to think that there is any choice, unless you make it a mean between good and evil.**

A96 No, instead what you say is ridiculous, for there is a certain kind of choice between good and evil. And therefore, when reason urges that which is less evil, either the will embraces that which is worse, as most often the time it does, or it allows itself to be ruled by reason. It really choses, but always evilly.

Q97 **But surely it is not the role of reason to urge evil.**

A97 Yes indeed, reason urges evil, for evil endows itself with the countenance of good so that it will be approved by reason. But the true rule for discovering good is found in the law of God, not from the corrupt reason of man. Therefore, even that which the natural man (as the apostle termed it) thinks is good, and desires as good, is said to be evil by the Spirit of God, as always stepping somewhat aside from that which is good. For certainly that which gushes out of an unclean pipe, still if now and then it is not as

1 Cor. 2:14

filthy as the filth of the pipe by itself, nevertheless, it is necessary that it be impure.

Q98 **Yet I do not understand how it is called free
which necessarily tends to only one of the
options.**

A98 Then remember that there is a difference
between compulsion and necessity, since many
necessary things are willed things, of which type
I think you at least will not deny the death of
Christ to be. But nothing is able to be compelled
and voluntary at the same time, not even in
those things which we do not want, as when
sailors have a shipwreck. Then, I ask you, look
a little nearer how you define freedom. For
which of these do you think is more free: he who
is in such a state that he can be a free man or
a slave, or he who is so free that he is not able
in any way to think of serving? Certainly, if you
consider free will to be that which is able to be
led to good and evil, you deprive both God and
angels of this evil, and us too after we will have
been received into heaven. Yes, and this also
could seem to be ambiguous: was the first man,
before hearing Satan, endowed with that judgement whereby he might deliberate on either
part? For how could evil come into question,
when it had not yet entered the world? So it
seems to me that Adam spontaneously strove
for only good with his whole mind and body
apart from any contrary thought or deliberation
at all, still less without deliberate choice; all
which things Satan has brought into the disposition of man, by introducing concupiscence in
us. Therefore, rightly was that tree named the
tree of the knowledge of good and evil, since
previously man only had known and desired
good; the fruit of which brought in his ruin, so
that men from that time on have not ceased to
debate over the ends of good and evil, although
they are enclosed within the limits of evil. The

John 8:36
Rom. 6:16
Rom. 8:15

conclusion is that he only is endowed with free will who is freed from the servitude of sin, which freedom will only be perfect when we are sinless in the other, eternal life, of which man has the Spirit of God as a certain pledge.

Q99 **Therefore, in the receiving of the first grace, men are merely sufferers of, not co-workers with the grace of God.**

A99 Yes, if you are only looking at it from the point of view of the order of causes, and the first initiation of grace, whereby the Lord reshapes us anew, it is necessary to admit that it comes wholly from God, who loved us first while we were still his enemies, and truly, we are only receivers of it. But if you consider the exact instance of time in which God works in us, at the same time and in the same moment it is given to us that we can want to receive it, and we do want to receive it, otherwise, grace would be in vain.[31]

Rom. 5:10
Titus 3:5
1 John 4:19

Therefore, he who fights the synergism of this type as if it were repugnant to the grace of God, they show their own inexperience in many ways, since this synergism is itself a gift of the grace of God, in such a way co-operating with it, so that in the order of causes it is the latter, as if it follows the effect that effects the cause; thus, all things accepted are wholly brought by the one grace of God. But still at the same time and in the same moment God brings it to pass that we may know through grace, and through grace we indeed do know; He brings it to pass that through grace we may will, and through grace we really do will; finally, He brings it to pass that through grace we might do, and through grace we really do. For the efficient cause of possibility cannot be called efficient in working, until the effect actually exists. Further, since neither the faculty of understanding nor of willing is taken from man by sin, as I said before, but only the faculty of understanding and willing rightly, it cannot be denied that there is in him at least a natural synergism, because when the first grace disposes, it is not received unless by will and intelligence, and men by nature are in general understanding and willing creatures - man, not as logs, but as one gifted with reason and will, receive the grace offered. And inasmuch as he does understand and will he is co-worker with God the Creator, from whom he obtains those natural faculties. Moreover, inasmuch as he understands and wills well, it should wholly be attributed to that foreign grace of God, whereby it happens that he prepares himself to make himself ready to think, will, and do rightly, when he receives the grace, and he actually does think, will, and do rightly.

Q100 **What must be understood concerning the effects of the first grace?**

A100 That the first grace is effectual, and is to be coupled with God's second grace, for we would immediately fall from the first, unless another followed, which makes the first effectual, and thus you must still progress from grace to grace.

Q101 **But it can hardly be denied that we, when we have received the first grace, work together with the rest of the graces that follow, and so the latter grace is attributed to the former merits.**

A101 Away with the name *merit*, which is diametrically opposed to grace, however much the semipelagian sophists argue to the contrary. He who denies that we are synergists of the first grace, denies the efficiency of the first grace. But that which I have said about the first synergism I say about those that follow. For that the first grace is so effectual to the extent that we use it well, is from the second grace; for if the second grace were not present, freely given and freely effectual, not only would we not move forward, we would digress to a far worse condition than

Rom. 4:4
1 Cor. 4:7

before. Finally, this synergism which, as I have said, is completely from the second grace - what does it have which might merit any compensation? Nothing at all, since even when we use it well (even then that is through grace, if it is closely inspected), we abuse it instead. Therefore, I confess that talents are added to the faithful servants; but again it is from mere grace that the works of the servants are approved, that they are considered faithful servants, and finally that rewards are given to them, which are owed them for no other reason, than that they were graciously promised, and graciously given.

Matt. 25:14

Rom. 4:5

Q102 **But I would eagerly wish to learn how this corruption is spread among the human race, by nature or by imitation.**

A102 Since you have satisfactorily established that corruption has entered, it is more imperative that you ask how it might be expelled. Nevertheless, here also, because of the many pernicious errors, I will try to satisfy you. Thus, I answer that evil is spread by nature, which afterwards is confirmed by imitation.

Q103 **How can you prove it?**

A103 With the many testimonies of scripture when you want, but especially by the argument of Paul taken from effects. For they also die who could not imitate Adam because they are not old enough, and death is the reward for sin.

Rom. 5:14
Rom. 6:23

Q104 **What if I should say that the first death, which is the separation of the body and soul, and later the resolution of the same body into its own elements, is natural. For all compound things are naturally subject to dissolution.**

A104 God Himself speaking to Moses will refute you. Besides this, this is not an argument of necessity. For although that which is compound is able to be dissolved by its own nature, actually it is not really dissolved, until the cause of its compounding ceases to sustain it. What do I say,

Gen. 2:17
Gen. 3:19
Rom. 5:12

then, that is absurd, when I say that man was in this way created of soul and body, and indeed that the body of man is composed from elements, so that the creator would have sustained them perpetually unless sin intervened.

Q105 I grant, then, that from mortal bodies arises mortal souls, but what is the corruption of the soul, unless perhaps you think that souls are also transferred?

A105 What opinions the many ancient writers had concerning this matter, I do not object to, nor do I wish to contend greatly concerning it, only so we might agree upon the natural spread of native sin. Nevertheless, I do not think this must be concealed, that the doctrine concerning the transfer of the soul seems to me to be very absurd, since either the whole soul or part of it would need to be transferred. If the whole, certainly it would be truly necessary that parts immediately be lost; if part only, how could any part of a simple essence be cut off?

Q106 If the soul is not from a corrupt father, but from the Father and Maker of spirits, how does it become corrupt? Is it from the infection of the body joined to it, as an ointment is affected the more quickly by an unclean container the better it is?

A106 It seems to me that this reasoning is able to satisfy all those of moderate intelligence. But in whatsoever way it is, it is enough, that Adam, just as he received the image of God for himself and his posterity, so he lost it for them, with God, just as he had threatened, deserting the souls immediately upon being created and infused into the body. From this it comes to pass that by nature all are born sons of wrath, clearly as the heirs of their fathers' corruption and guilt.

Rom. 5:12

Q107 Therefore, now let us return to the remedy of that evil, which is receiving Christ by faith

alone. I want you to explain to me what you mean by apprehension, ingrafting, incorporation, and fellowship with Christ.

A107 He who imagines any joining or linking of the substances themselves, or whatever way they dream it to be, they are hallucinating and are judging spiritual and mystical things in fleshly terms. Again he who makes the only operation and efficacy of Christ to be that of which we become partakers, does not seem to have sufficiently expended the express testimonies of scripture, in which Christ Himself is distinctly said to be given in us. Therefore, there are two things that must be established in order that we might understand what this communication is: the first is, that Christ Himself becomes ours by the kindness of the Father, so that all who believe can say, this thing (namely, that Christ is the Son of God manifest in the flesh) is mine by a free gift of the Father, so I can to use it for enjoyment.

Isaiah 9:5
Rom. 8:32
1 Cor. 10:16
Eph. 5:30
John 17:11,
21,22

Q108 **Here I ask that you permit me to infer that he who speaks in the manner which you just described is lord of the thing given; but, we are not lords of Christ Himself, are we? Is He not our Lord?**

A108 If anyone denies that Jesus Christ is our Lord, and with the highest right since the Father both gave us to Him, and He Himself redeemed us at a great cost, let Him be anathema. Therefore, when I say that He is ours who believe, I do not mean there is any power given to us over Him, but that He was given and born for us. For example, a man marries a wife, to whom the wife must be obedient and serving, but in such a way that the wife is able to say on the one hand, just as I am the wife of this man to whom my father gave me, so that he has authority over me, on the other hand he is married to me, who gave himself to me to enjoy, in order that he might

John 13:3
John 17:10
1 Cor. 6:20
1 Cor. 7:23

love me and cherish me as a wife - which similitude you know the prophets and apostles often used to explain this communication. The other point of this communication is that He becomes ours in such a way that no joining of bodies, either natural or artificial, is able to be compared with it, yet not in a way that one certain person or substance forms from His substance or person, or from our substance or person (all which things are crass comments, and utterly foreign from the King of heaven), but only in this way: that this spiritual energy becomes more certain, more joined, and more efficacious in us. And yet this is certain, that He becomes ours in such a way that He truly becomes one with us, and no head and members of a body cleave so firmly together, as this joining of Christ is firm and close, so that we become flesh of his flesh, and bone of his bone, but wholly in a spiritual and mystical way.

Rom 7:1ff
1 Cor. 11:2
Eph. 5:15

Eph. 5:30

Q109 Explain, please, why you call it spiritual.

A109 I call it spiritual, not in respect to that which is communicated of Him (for certainly it is with the whole humanity, not by spirit alone, that Christ is communicated to us) or as if this union were imaginary, and consisted in thought alone, resting not on the things itself, and not as if we are said to become one with Christ only by reason of consent, as when Luke writes that the believers were one heart and one mind, but because all this apprehension is of spirit and faith, and the Holy Spirit is the one by whose linking these things which are so far divided in space, come together. Therefore, as Christ is the head in this spiritual copulation, and the church is the body, it draws spiritual life from him its head. Thus, the belief in the actual coalition of the very substances themselves (concerning which many men have contended so perniciously for a long time, from whence later the

Acts 4:32

Eph. 4:15-16

monster of transubstantiation and consubstantiation were drawn) is a crass comment of a vain mankind, in no way consistent with the spiritual life or the truth of the body of Christ, nor the analogy of faith.[32]

Q110 Indeed I hear that Christ is received by the faithful by faith; I hear that the church is spiritually coupled with its head by the bond of the Holy Spirit; but I do not perceive any better, how these things that are so different are united.

Eph. 5:32

A110 I agree. For it is not in vain that Paul exclaimed that this is a great mystery. Rightly, then, does one warn that we should instead labor to feel Christ living in us, than seek the rationale of this communication in us, which surpasses our capacity, although we know it is spiritual and that it is done by the instrument of faith.

Q111 What if we say that Christ is communicated to us only in respect to his energy and efficacy? And what if we say that the passage of Paul, "We are members of his body from his flesh and bone," refers to Christ's incarnation?

Eph. 5:30

A111 The Scriptures most plainly say concerning the communication of Christ Himself that we draw life from our union with Him, rather than that it can be applied to his energy alone. For He is the foundation of both the effectual fellowship and of the benefit of imputation, which is illustrated by Christ Himself from the analogy of bodily nourishment. For like as you receive nourishment from food necessary to sustaining life, it is necessary that it be your own also, so you can eat it. Likewise, in order that we may draw from Christ the juice of eternal life, it is necessary that He be taken hold of by us by the mouth of faith, and to be spiritually digested in us. Moreover, the passage of Paul concerning the assumption of the human nature cannot be applied in this instance. For according to that anyone can rightly say, that they are members

Eph. 5:32

of Christ, which the apostle referred properly of the Church alone, which also the analogy of bodily wedlock requires. For every man is not one flesh with every woman, but is joined only with one whom he married for a wife, and the woman is only one flesh with the man whose wife she is. Therefore, this copulation into one flesh is not of nature, but of covenant, and so also is our union with Christ into one spirit. Finally, if the apostle wished to signify what you say, he rather should have said that Christ is of our flesh and of our bones, if He joined Himself to us by His incarnation, however we are joined to Him by faith.[33]

Q112 Continue, please, and show me what we receive from Christ being spiritually connected with us through faith, as you have said.

A112 Again, even though we walk into an abyss whose width, length, and depth, surpasses our understanding (as the apostle says), we know so far as the spirit with which we are endowed examines the depths of God. How could He who has not spared His only Son, the apostle said, but has given Him for us all, not give us all things with Him? Therefore, I respond that all things necessary to salvation flow forth into us from Christ by our apprehending Him through faith.

Eph. 1:18ff
Eph. 3:8-10

Q113 But I want you to explain to me what those things are in particular, if possible.

A113 Therefore, I respond that some things are Christ's in such a way that they always cling in Him alone, and do not become ours other than by imputation, of which sort are those things He performed for our sake, namely, that having become under the law He completed all righteousness, and suffered the penalties owed for our sins; both of which the apostle knew by the name of obedience. And some things so reside in Christ that still the power and energy of them

Gal. 4:4
Matt. 3:15
Rom. 5:19

Phil. 2:8
Rom. 8:3,4

spread into us, of which type is that highest purity of the human nature in Christ, clothed with all gifts without measure, which not only becomes ours through imputation, but also is the fount and origin of our regeneration and of all following spiritual gifts.

Q114 What is imputation?
A114 The benefit of God the Father whereby He deigns to reckon that obedience of Christ as ours, as if we ourselves had fulfilled the law, and made satisfaction for our sins.

Q115 But is this consistent with the nature of God, that one should be held righteous by an alien righteousness?
A115 This righteousness is alien inasmuch as it is outside us and in another subject, namely, residing in Christ. But it is not alien inasmuch as that subject Himself, namely Christ, is ours. And also, He is so much ours that He is made spiritually one with us through faith.

Q116 No, if He has become one with us, it seems now that anything He has in Himself, is really ours, and not just through imputation.
A116 Certainly, assuming a real copulation and uniting of the very substance of Christ with ours (which follows from the dogma of them who teach that the flesh and blood of Christ are eaten by our very mouths and conveyed in us), that which you say follows, from which one can see how greatly the doctrines of transubstantiation and consubstantiation oppose the doctrine of the imputation of righteousness, just as much as it removes the truth of Christ's flesh. But I have said already that Christ is really communicated to us, but this mystery is merely spiritual, whose link is the Holy Spirit. However the aim it takes is not for any coalition of the substance or persons themselves (for what purpose would that be?), but that spiritual life should thus flow

Eph. 4:15-16
Eph. 5:23

down from Christ the mystical head to the body, the mystical subject.

Q117 Let us return to imputation.

A117 I return and I say, just as there is any defect of righteousness in us, and fallingness to sin, it is outside of Christ, and nevertheless is imputed to Christ. So on the other hand the obedience of Christ is outside of us, that is, inherent to Christ alone, but is imputed to us. However, this is the foundation of this imputation, that He is one with us, and we are one with Him (by spiritual manner and method, as we have said), so that He was not a sinner in Himself but in us, and we are not made righteous in ourselves, but in Him.

Q118 But faith is said to have been imputed to Abraham for righteousness, not by this obedience of Christ.

Rom. 4:3

A118 Know this, that those things which are subordinate are not contrary. Faith is said to be imputed for righteousness, since it is the instrument whereby that obedience, by the imputation of which we are made righteous, is apprehended. For which reason also we are said to be justified by faith, inasmuch as it apprehends the obedience of Christ by whose imputation we are declared righteous.

Rom. 5:1-9

Q119 Still some doubt remains, how your saying that Christ is apprehended by faith, is consistent with that which you formerly declared, when you affirmed that when Christ is apprehended by faith all gifts flow forth into us. But it seems to follow that either faith is not a gift of God, or that your latter statement is false. For faith most surely must go before the apprehension, if Christ is apprehended by faith.

A119 The beginning of our salvation is from God, who chose us in Christ before we were born, even before the foundations of the world were laid;

Eph. 1:4
Rom. 3:24

2 Tim. 1:9
1 John 4:19

and He first loved and knew us after we were born, although we were not yet actually ingrafted and given to Christ, but were to be given and grafted. Therefore, if you consider the exact moment of time, we both believe and apprehend Christ who is offered to us at the same time. For the cause is not able to actually be working, unless at the same time the effect comes forth. But if you consider the order of causes, I confess that the rudiment of true faith is before the apprehension of Christ, and therefore not actually given to those who have been ingrafted, but to those about to be grafted. Nevertheless, it does not follow hence that faith is not given to us in Christ, since the heavenly Father, acquiescing in His only Son, does not then for the first time consider us in Christ, but He elected us in Him, and He knew and loved us, even before the foundation of the world, and while we yet hated Him. Likewise Christ Himself also first takes us so that we might take Him.

Phil. 3:12
Rom. 5:6,8,10

Then that which is begun in us through grace, so that we are ingrafted into Christ, and therefore according to the order of causes, is before the apprehension of Christ Himself - it is increased and confirmed in us by the same grace in the same Christ whom we have apprehended now through faith.

Q120 **Therefore, what are the things which we attain in Christ?**

A120 Paul plainly, yet briefly, concluded this whole argument, when he said that Christ was made, by God the Father, wisdom, justification, sanctification, and redemption for us.

1 Cor. 1:30

Q121 **What do you mean, He was made wisdom for us?**

A121 The same thing which Zechariah means when he says that his son John the Baptist is sent in order to show us the knowledge of salvation, that is, Christ Himself. For this is true wisdom,

Luke 1:77

Col. 2:2-3

which Christ showed when He revealed Himself to men, which also the Father, with a loud voice, testified from heaven saying, hear Him.

Matt. 17:5

Q122 But do you reckon this among the gifts we receive from Christ?

A122 I mean that Christ Himself is given to us as the only teacher of that true and inborn wisdom, as He teaches us about Himself. For He Himself is both the teacher and that which is taught. Therefore, among the gifts of Christ the first and primary is that He gives Himself to us, when He provides us with the knowledge of Himself.

Q123 What does Paul mean by justification in this passage?

A123 It is that whereby we are made righteous, that is, so perfect, whole, faultless, and unblamable, that God, who is wholly pure, not only fully abolishes in us that which is unclean and offensive, but also seems to find abundant delight in this human nature, so that He willingly crowns it with eternal life. Finally, of that righteousness by which a man is accounted righteous before God, the law of God is a certain, invariable rule and norm. And the law not only prohibits not doing things, with the threat of eternal death added, but also requires the perfect love of God and neighbor. Therefore, in order that someone might be righteous before God, two things are necessarily required, namely, the absence of all sin, and total fulfillment of all righteousness according to the law.

Eph. 1:4

James 2:8

Q124 But that has never been found in a mortal man.

A124 Except in Christ, who not only never sinned, but also completely fulfilled the law.

Q125 Tell me, please, was Christ perfectly righteous from the very moment of conception?

A125 Yes, inasmuch as He was God, who was not only righteous from eternity, but also, righteousness itself, that is, the highest and most perfect

Matt. 1:20

Luke 1:35

purity. Moreover, inasmuch as He was man, He was from the very moment of the conception of His flesh, endowed with excellent holiness even

Matt. 3:15
John 17:4
John 19:30

above the angels themselves. But now, by the term righteousness we mean, that which is a consequence of the perfect keeping of God's law, which Christ did not have until that time

Phil. 3:9,10

He had completed all the work commanded to Him. For this is the righteousness by the impu-

Pet. 2:22

tation of which we are justified, not that essential righteousness which is of the Godhead, nor that habitual righteousness, that is to say, the purity of Christ's flesh, concerning which we will deal with separately - which when Osiander[34] did not distinguish, he shamefully hallucinated.

Q126 But I do not yet see how this righteousness is sufficient. For since we not only do not keep the law, but also we are covered with infinite sins, how will we be reckoned as if we never have sinned, that is, not contaminated with sins, unless first the spots of our sins are removed? However, that is not able to happen unless the penalties are paid.

A126 You are correct. Therefore, what I have said concerning Christ not only not violating the law, but also perfectly and fully keeping it, understand that in this way He made satisfaction for all the sins of believers. For everyone is bound by the law of God to love God and his neighbor, not indefinitely, but definitely, that is, taking account of His own calling. As, for example, if a magistrate should love God only as some private citizen does, he is said not to do his duty, because he is bound to love God as a magistrate; which example must be understood in relation to all other kinds of vocations. Moreover, Christ was sent in order to pay the debts for our sin on our behalf, which He surely performed by His entire

Phil. 2:8

life, but especially by His own sacrifice, being

obedient to the Father even to death, the death of the cross. Therefore, by living through suffering, and by offering Himself on our behalf, He both fulfilled the law for us, and made satisfaction for our sins.

Q127 But Christ, inasmuch as He has become man, seems to have been obligated by nature to keep the righteousness of the law, that is, to perfectly love God and neighbor, since this law is imposed on the very nature of man. Therefore, He seems to have fulfilled the law, not for us, but for Himself, so that He could purchase life for Himself, which thing is not able to be said concerning the penalties paid for our sins by Him.

A127 Even if we say that Christ according to the flesh merited for Himself eternal life by the fulfillment of the law to which He was bound, still it is not absurd to say that the force of this merit is so great, that it flows forth to believers also. But the former statement cannot be justified. For since this humanity was united to the Logos by personal union, and in such a way indeed that it was even most holy in itself, who thinks (if this assumed nature can be viewed outside of the work of the mediatorship, which is not joined to the humanity in and of itself, but enjoined to the Son by the Father by His own good will, and willingly received by the Son), who, I ask, thinks that anything could be wanting in this assumed humanity, so that it would not be immediately most worthy of the eternal life, from the very first moment of that union? Therefore, this obligation of the flesh to keep the law is not one of the nature itself, but of will, not simply because Christ is a man, but because He became man for us; which condition He undertook and performed, not for Himself, for He is already by full right most blessed, but for us, on whose behalf He willed to become under

Gal. 4:45

the law so that He might redeem those who were under the law. Furthermore, see how uncertain it is which you said last of all concerning the satisfaction for our sins. For that is the most important part of His obedience or fulfillment of the law, as we proved a little bit before. Therefore, if He fulfilled the law for Himself, it is necessary that you confess that He died for His own sake also.

Q128 Therefore, you say that we are justified before God, that is, held to be and declared righteous, because the obedience of Christ is imputed to us, which consists of two distinct parts, the satisfaction for our sins, and the full observance of all legal righteousness.[35]

A128 That is correct.

Q129 Therefore, to what purpose is Christ made our sanctification? For certainly he who is held to be righteous is also considered holy.

A129 He who is righteous, the same needs also to be holy, but not contrawise, unless a new grace comes forth from the former, according as we formerly defined the term righteous in this argument, namely, for him who is not held as a transgressor of the law, since his sins are expiated in Christ, but also has fulfilled the law in Him. In brief, I call holiness the goodness and purity of one's person; and that this righteousness, concerning which now we speak and by which the believers are termed righteous in themselves, is not the imputed righteousness, but is the result of that holiness; so that the former is a tree, and the latter is the fruit of it.[36] In this way Adam was created holy, good, and pure, and would also have become righteous, if he kept the law given by condition.

1 John 3:9

Q130 But all men are by nature corrupt.

A130 Again, all are by nature corrupt except Christ the second Adam, conceived of the Holy Spirit, so that the human nature not only received in Him a lost purity, but also in infinite ways it was elevated into a more sublime level of goodness. For the former Adam was only created in the image of God, but the latter is even God Himself, since He is sustained by the eternal Son of God in Him, who indescribably made the assumed nature holy, and so became sanctification for us.

Q131 But why do you call Christ the second Adam?

A131 Because just as Adam was created and from him all men spring by natural propagation, so Christ assumed the human nature on the condition that all who believe in Him might be spiritually regenerated through grace.

Q132 Then is it not enough to be born once in the natural way.

A132 Altogether, in regards to this life, also in respect to which, it would be foolish to think that we are born more than once. But when Adam rendered himself subject to both deaths, both for him and for his posterity, it was necessary for us either to perish, or entirely by some other condition to be reborn into eternal life. For that reason a second Adam was given to us, from whom holiness and eternal life flow down into us spiritually and graciously, just as naturally and bodily sin and death are in us from the first Adam.

Q133 Therefore, explain fully this sanctification of ours in Christ.

A133 Something is said to be sanctified which is segregated from common pollution, so that it is most pure, and wholly consecrated to God the greatest adversary of all filth. Therefore, in this way our nature is sanctified in Christ from the very moment of conception, and so He sanctifies us. Furthermore it happens in two ways. First, as I have said, we are reckoned righteous by the imputed righteousness of Christ fully before God, not in ourselves, but in Him to whom we are united through faith. So also I say that our persons, by the imputation of His perfect holiness and integrity, are reckoned holy and whole and thus acceptable to the Father, not in ourselves, but in Christ. Finally, the force and energy of this most pure holiness which is in the flesh of Christ, I say it flows also into us by the working of the Holy Spirit in us, so that we become holy in ourselves, that is, segregated from the defilements of this world, and we serve God in spirit and body; which benefit in the scriptures is often termed sanctification, regeneration, illumination, new man, new creature, and spirituality.

Q134 **Therefore, you say that this latter sanctification is not something outside of us, and is not ours by imputation alone, but is a new endowment truly ingrafted and clinging in us, by the mere grace of the heavenly Father, and by the power of the Holy Spirit, diffused in us.**

A134 I say so.

Q135 **Therefore, to what end is the other sanctification of our nature which is imputed to us?**

A135 Because this sanctification which is inherent in us is unfinished in us, as is apparent by the perpetual warfare between the flesh and the spirit in us, even in the best men. Therefore, in order that our persons might be acceptable to God, and consequently so that that which comes forth from us might please Him (for the life of the saints is as a kind of continual offering up of oneself, to which the apostle exhorted us), another sanctification must intervene; clearly, another which is most full and whole in Christ, in whom our most kind Father, looking, might acquiesce, He who is a perpetual enemy to all uncleanness, and is the most just and merciful.

Rom. 7:25

Gal. 5:17

Rom. 12:1

Q136 But why does He not completely sanctify us immediately?

A136 No, instead marvel at His goodness, in that He instills any little drop of regenerating grace in man. Yet why He defers the full sanctification of us into another age, there are many reasons, and chiefly two. One, because we are of little faith, and therefore, as much as is in us, we impede the inworking of the Holy Spirit. The second, so that, as we are saved by grace alone, and not by works, he who glories, should glory only in God. For if this sanctification were complete in us, our righteousness would also be complete, or inherent in us, and then Christ would not be wholly and properly our Saviour, but only the tool and instrument for disposing us in such a way that we might justify ourselves by our own righteousness, which is plainly the foul and detestable error of the Semi-Pelagian Sophists.[37]

1 Cor. 1:13

Q137 You say, then, that between our sanctification and our righteousness, there is this proportion, that how great the one is, so is the other also.

A137 Altogether. For true sanctification is not able to be idle; and of what kind a fruitbearing tree is, so also is the fruit of that tree. Therefore, since our intellect is partly illumined with the knowledge of the true God, we also know in part; since we partly assent to the promise of God, and apply it to ourselves, therefore we believe in part; since our will is partly unchanged, therefore we will and do rightly only in part.

Luke 6:44

1 Cor. 13:12

Q138 What do you mean, ''partly?''

A138 That is, not perfectly, but only to the extent that we are regenerated, so that in the same subject (although in various respects), there is purity and uncleanness, light and darkness, faith and unbelief, good will, and will lacking good, spirit and flesh.

Q139 What do you mean by ''spirit?''

A139 All the faculties of men, both superior and inferior, to the degree that they are sanctified or regenerated.

Q140 And what do you call flesh.

A140 In an unregenerate man, I call the whole man flesh, completely, inside and out, from head to toe; but in a regenerate man, all the faculties of him to the degree that they are not sanctified or regenerated.

1 John 3:6 **Q141 But John says that the children of God do not sin.**

A141 The same person says that they lie who say that
1 John 1:8 they have no sin. Therefore, they are said not to sin, because the sin that dwells in them does not rule them. For the spirit contends in them against the flesh, and eventually wins. There-
Rom. 7:15 fore, the regenerate alone can rightly say, I do the evil which I do not want to do, and I do not do the good which I want to do.

Q142 Even the natural reasoning in any man, even an unregenerate man, often fights against his lusts. And in this you know our virtues rest - that the unreasonable part of the mind is subjected to the reasonable.

A142 What must be thought concerning the philosophical virtues I have already responded. I grant that there is a certain wariness, a certain conscionableness left in man to reprove, and to a certain degree, impede the lack of discipline
Rom. 1:20 of the affections, so that every man is inexcusa-
Rom. 3:11,12 ble. Therefore, the things which the peripatetics write concerning the philosophical distribution, as if of the parts of the soul, and concerning a middle state, not only do I reprehend as false, but also I praise and admire them as remains of the image of God. But I say that the distribution of the parts of man is far different, as the Holy Spirit teaches us: natural and spiritual, interior

and exterior man, old and new man, flesh and spirit opposing one another; and in those terms by which vice is noted, He also means that very guiding part of the mind of which the philosophers speak; and finally, it also includes whatever men have by nature outside of the grace of regeneration.

Q143 Is reason, then, not reason?

A143 Yes it is, and indeed it always becomes better sighted by searching, yet it always falls short, until it is regenerated; for first even when it knows and discerns the good, it nevertheless does not know and discern as it needs and ought, on account of the original corruption which the philosophers are not ever able to suspect. Then, in many even serious matters, not only does it not discern the truth, but also utterly and of set purpose fights the truth.

Q144 Please confirm these things with examples.

A144 I will do it. Although the philosophers write many things notably and very excellently concerning God the highest good, nevertheless, which of them knows by his own insight that the one substance of God is in three persons? And yet only this notion of God, the highest good, is true and salvific.

John 5:23
John 17:8

Q145 But still a man named Trismegistus, and certain Platonists, are said to have taught some such thing.

A145 Indeed, it can be that some men have known obscurely concerning this mystery delivered over by the Patriarchs and written in the sacred books: but away with the follies of those men who seek this truth in the writings of the philosophers! For when they are about to explain the nature of God, after they have said many things, how suddenly do the best of them (as rightly the apostle has said) fall away. From whence are these many gods? From whence is this dis-

Rom. 1:18

tribution of the godhead into major and minor deities? From whence is the ragings of the Epicureans? From whence is the stoical necessity which constrains the godhead itself? From whence is the deliriousness of Aristotle, who dreams that the world is eternal, and who removes particular providence, and the other innumerable follies later refuted by Aristotle himself? To whom do we attribute the beginnings of all superstitions except to this overruler? Now, if we come down to man, which of the philosophers knows himself, being ignorant of the origin of the first man and the fall itself? Yes, what can be imagined more absurdly, more insanely, or more monstrous, than the opinions some men do not cease to attribute to Aristotle, the sharpest of all the philosophers, that there is only one soul in all mankind? For these wise men do not even agree concerning the immortality of the soul, and they do battle often concerning the affections. And if we come down to the mutual duties of man among men, how many things not only absurdly, but also evilly and shamefully, have the legislatures who are greatly praised by all of the people, established: which of them ever thought of the true remedy against the disorder of the affections? And it is no marvel, since they never knew the cause or effects of this deadly disease. Therefore, you see that reason itself also, while it remains natural, is blind in serious matters. How many things are there in which reason is not only blind, but also completely insane? For besides that, each one defends so stubbornly the few errors which I have enumerated from many, so that he does not allow himself to be taught more correctly, that the world was created from nothing, that the Word became flesh, that a child came from a virgin, that we are considered righteous by the righteousness of another, the resurrection of the dead, and many other things not only does reason deny, but also loathes and scorns. Yes, and if you press her more, finally furiously she tramples the entire heavenly wisdom under foot, unless from the grace of God she is made spiritual. And then even she does not cease to wrestle against the known wisdom, inasmuch as she is not changed. Therefore, you see, I hope, that what I was saying is true.

Q146 But among you theologians, although you are spiritual, there is still some disagreement.

A146 Indeed, this is not the fault of the Holy Scriptures, in which plainly and clearly enough the true dogmas of religion are explained; but it must be attributed to this same reason, which is both blind and stubborn. But I did not say that we are completely regenerated (because if that were true, we would consent in one truth on all points), but only partly. Therefore, I do not deny that the remains of that ignorant and stubborn nature still abides, but they are abolished little by little.

Q147 Therefore, let us profess that whatever is in us of sincere knowledge, or right judgement, or righteous desire, is from the mere grace of the heavenly Father in His Son. But will you not admit that this righteousness inherent in us is righteousness, and thus pleasing to God.

Matt. 7:17

A147 I concede that it is righteousness - for the good tree produces good fruit - but by way of comparison, if it is compared to fruits that are rotten. But if the very best works of even the holiest of men, should be tried according to God's will, that is, the law, I say they are sins not fully set against the law as much as adultery, stealing and lying, but lacking that degree of goodness the law requires. Thus we must rest ourselves in the one obedience of Christ, imputed to us through faith, as that which alone is perfect and absolute at all points.

Q148 No, by what right does God require from man, whom by his very nature, of which God Himself is the author, He knows is not sufficiently able to keep?

A148 That we do not keep the law, arises not by nature, which willed and was very much able to yield to the creator (in whose image it was created) that which He required and which it owed, since it was created to the same purpose. But from the spontaneous corruption of the nature did this spring, which makes it so happen so that no one knows the debt, and much less wants or is able to keep it. No, all do nothing but increase the debts. But (if we may speak as men) does he who is not able to pay cease to be a debtor? Furthermore, although the Creator requires it from us by the highest right, both that, and perhaps more, to us believing in His Son who was given in grace, likewise He will freely bestow the very faith, whereby we will perceive the offered gift. Who, then, would not rather adore the immense goodness of the Father, than contend with Him?

Rom. 5:15,16

Q149 Therefore, may eternal praise and glory be to God the highest good. Still, let it be my right to question this: at least this inherent righteousness, inasmuch as it takes account of righteousness, should please God, who delights in righteousness.

A149 I do not, I think, perceive your craftiness, but that of Satan. For since he is not able to utterly take away the glory of our salvation from Christ, therefore he tries at least to tear away some small bit of it, which he has obviously done, if he persuades men what the Sophists write, namely, that the righteousness of Christ is incomplete without our righteousness. Thus accept this: God loves righteousness to the extent that whatever small amount of righteousness and purity one has, in some measure He approves it; yet

Psalms 5:5
Rom. 2:9

this is done from His infinite goodness, not from any merit of this kind of feigned righteousness. In this way He approved the repentance of the Ninevites and Achabus, which was not a true repentance, but a kind of humiliation under the powerful hand of God. For it is so good that it even benefits the indignant, not to speak of them who in what way soever are affected by a sense of the majesty itself. Therefore, God much more delights in the works of the regenerate, although they are imperfect; but first I say that these works of the regenerate please, not on account of any worthiness of them, but from the mere grace of the Father, who overlooks what lacks of righteousness, and who approves what proceeds from the Holy Spirit. Finally, I deny that the cause of our justification, and also eternal life, must be attributed to these works, which please God only out of mere grace. For this stands, the righteous will live by faith, and eternal life is the gift of God.

Rom. 1:17

Rom. 6:23

Heb. 12:2

Q149 But if they please God, they seem in some way (at least) to be worthy.

A149 This is a most false consequence. For God is not able to approve (even of covenant)[38] another righteousness as worthy of that name (unless He wants to contradict himself, which is a sin to say) than that which responds to the law exactly. Thus, you should have gathered instead that the works of the unregenerate please God, even though they are imperfect. Therefore, God is very merciful.

Q150 Besides this, everywhere there is mention of wages and compensation.

A150 The term *wages* has a wider scope than that of eternal life, and it is certain that temporal blessings also are rendered to the impious, however indignant they are, from God's liberality. Then, whether you apply the term wages to eternal life or to other benefits, it still does not follow that

Rom. 4:4

a debt is paid. No, this greatly commends the mercy of God, that the undue reward, which is bestowed from the mere grace in Christ, is nevertheless termed *wage*, so that we, although *Luke 17:10* we are unprofitable servants (for who adds anything to God?), still know that we in no way have made believe our work.[39] Finally, although these wages are freely promised and freely given, still it is given to the one who works, and therefore is called wages.

Q151 If to the one who works, then it is given to him for his works.

A151 No, if it is given, certainly it is not paid as a debt. Again, there is a great difference between giving to the worker and giving to the works. Therefore, I say well that eternal life is given to those who work, since faith is estimated by its effects, and righteousness by faith; but eternal life not paid for their works. After this manner it is necessary to explain this passage: "Everyone *2 Cor. 5:10* must be judged according to those things which he has done in the body," and other such passages.

Q152 Why so?

A152 Because good works do not justify, but follows the one who believes and is already justified in Christ, just as good fruits do not make a tree good, but a tree is known to be good by its good *Matt. 7:17,18* fruits.

Q153 But a little before you drew good works out of sanctification, not out of righteousness.

A153 I agree. But no one is justified by the imputed *Rom. 15:16* righteousness of Christ, except he also is sanctified by the Spirit.

Q154 Therefore, you say that good works are necessary to salvation?

A154 If faith is necessary to salvation, and works necessarily flow out of true faith, (as that which cannot be idle), certainly also it follows, that good works are necessary to salvation,[40] yet not as the cause of salvation (for we are justified, and thus live, by faith alone in Christ), but as something necessarily attached to true faith. Just as Paul says, they are God's children, who are led by the Spirit of God; and John, that he is righteous who works righteousness; and James also, explaining not by what method we are justified, but, from whence true faith and justification are known, proves by the example of Abraham that they are not justified who demonstrate no works of faith. For in this way James is reconciled with Paul, so that it is plain that they are contentious who condemn the necessity of good works as a false doctrine.

Rom. 8:14

1 John 3:7

James 2:21

Q155 What if someone is not endowed with faith until the very moment of death itself. For this seems to have happened to the thief hanging on the cross. What kind of good works will someone of this type have brought forth?

A155 No, the faith of that thief was in that brief time unspeakably active, for he rebuked the blasphemes and wickedness of the other thief, he detested his own crimes, and with a plain and marvelous faith he acknowledged Christ as the eternal king while he was in the very disgrace of the cross; as all the disciples kept silent, he invoked him as his Saviour, and finally he openly reproved the cruelties and ungodly voices of the Jews. Moreover, the acknowledgement of sin, the invocation of God the Father in Christ, and thanksgiving, are the most excellent works of the first Table,[41] which cannot be separated from faith in any man. Yet someone who is prevented by death is not able to demonstrate any of the works of the second table. Nevertheless, faith is not to be considered idle in him, since although it does not have charity joined in deed, it has it joined in potentiality.

Luke 23:40ff

Q156 I still have one hesitation. How is it that some-

one is condemned by evil works, if one is not justified by good works?

A156 But the reason is clear, since even the lightest sin is worthy, not of the highest penalties in eternal death, but of eternal death itself, which is in general the payment for sin. But no righteousness is able to worthily merit eternal life, except such as the law requires, a perfect and sound state. Give to me someone who fulfills the law completely, even as there is none who is not a transgressor of the law, and I will concede that argument to you.

Rom. 6:32

Rom. 3:20

Q157 **Therefore, you say that there will be unequal punishments of the damned?**

A157 Although one must inquire concerning this thing very soberly, still I do not say it timidly. For besides that the very rationale of justice requires that since all sins are not equal among themselves, except inasmuch as they match in general; he who sins more grieviously will be punished more grieviously (for it is a paradox of the Stoics, not of the Christians, whereby all sins are considered equal). Christ even testified to it expressly, saying that it will be a more tolerable condition for the Sodomites in the day of judgement, than for those by whom he was rejected.

Matt. 10:15

Q158 **Therefore, unequal also will be the glories of them who will be saved.**

A158 Altogether, for the rationale of contraries requires it. And what the apostle said, that those who have sown sparsely, will reap sparsely, does not seem to refer to temporal blessings only.

2 Cor. 9:6

Q159 **But from sowing comes forth reaping. Therefore, righteousness and life come from good works themselves.**

A159 No, never should similitudes be drawn further than the nature of the things that are being discussed will bear, and the purpose of him who uses the similitudes. Otherwise, infinite absurdities and falsities will follow, which when unskilled interpreters do not pay attention, many inept and false things necessarily come forth. But in that place the apostle makes an analogy of works and glory, not, however, of the cause of glory. For everywhere he constantly defends the fact that righteousness is a mere gift of God apart from the works of the law, and is not paid as a debt, but is imputed to the believers as grace.

Q160 He means we are to keep the works of the ceremonial law.

A160 A ridiculous response. For that opposition of debt and grace cannot fare well, unless all the works of the law are excluded without one exception; as the other arguments of Paul directly bent against the very law of the Decalog itself I will pass by. Bent, I say, not to vituperate the law (which is the insanity of the Manicheans), but so that he might strip it of the power of justifying. Again, I beg of you, if a righteousness which is accepted by works is to be brought forth, why do you exclude the ceremonies rightly used? For certainly they are comprehended in the fourth precept of the Decalogue itself, and as long as they were rightly used, they were most excellent works.

Rom. 4:4

Rom. 7:7

Q161 But the ceremonies were abolished by the advent of Christ.

A161 I agree that they are abolished, because they are completed in Christ. But the matter itself declares that where Paul disputes concerning the causes of justification, his arguments do not tend to indicate that he teaches that the ceremonies are abolished, but that salvation rests in the righteousness of Christ alone imputed to believers, with Abraham and David, among others, given as examples.

Q162 Then let us say that only the good works preceding the grace of justification are excluded by Paul.

A162 No less inept is this response. For besides the fact that the apostle clearly puts forth examples and testimonies of righteous men, namely Abraham and David; so that I may pass over his other reasons grounded on the very nature of the law, what madness is it to work on excluding those things which do not exist? For to establish the good works of them who are not justified, is no less foolish than if someone should say that good fruits cannot come from a tree until it begins to be good.

Rom. 4:6-10

Q163 But if the wages of eternal life is not owed from the worthiness of the works themselves, still it is at least due from the covenant.

A163 What covenant do you mean?

Q164 The covenant of the law: Do this, and you will live, and if you want to enter life, keep the commandments.

A164 This covenant is understood in terms of the threatening which is set against the promise. Moreover, it holds, by the testimony of the apostle himself, he who does not remain in all things which are written in the book of the law, so that he keeps them, is cursed. Now the law requires perfect love. But no one besides Christ alone fully keeps the law. Therefore, life is owed to Christ alone by the covenant; moreover, to us, to whom He is given by mere grace, life is given from the same by mere grace.

Gal. 3:10

Q165 Therefore, why do you call them good works, if they do not promote eternal life?

A165 Certainly the Latin theologians, even the old ones, used the word "merit" for "obtain;" and the word "merit" for a good work, which you never find in the sacred Scriptures. But although the works of the regenerate are not so good, that they merit eternal life, nevertheless they are good, inasmuch as they proceed from the good Spirit of God, and from a heart cleansed by faith. And again, they are good, because the Lord is glorified by them, our neighbor is helped; and we also perceive the excellent fruit of them, because they are testimonies to us of our faith, and consequently our election.

Q166 **Therefore, let thus far suffice concerning both parts of sanctification. It still remains what the apostle said, that Christ has become our redemption.**

A166 The Apostle calls redemption in that passage, not the very action of redeeming, but the effect, that is, the end to which the justification and sanctification leads us, that we are redeemed by Christ from death, and therefore we become participants of eternal life, whose pledge and earnest money we have even in this life, the Holy Spirit by whom we are sealed.

Q167 **But David grounded this redemption and blessing in the remission of sins. Why, then, do you also add the imputation of the sanctification inherent in Christ Himself, and His fulfillment of the law?**

A167 What if I should confront you with these passages: Blessed are the pure in heart, Blessed are those who are blameless in the way, and other of this type; would you gather that from this the remission of sins is excluded? I think not. Thus, now and then even our sanctification is meant by the term justification, since they are necessarily a united concept. Therefore, what if I should respond like this: now and then mention is made of the remission of sins only, not to exclude the other parts of blessing, but because they are quietly understood with it? But if you urge me further, I would respond that other things are signified by the remission of sins. For who would deny that original sin is in need of expiation? Therefore, it is understood in the remission of sins. Likewise, who says that he only must be a sinner who does something prohibited, and not also him who does not fulfill which is commanded of him? Therefore, sin is also not to fulfill the law, which also needs to be forgiven. There remains the sins, which are works done contrary to the law, concerning which there is not controversy, but that they must be expiated. Moreover, all these things are remitted by the satisfaction of Christ imputed to us all. Now, let us come to the term remission. A man is said to properly remit a debt, who freely and utterly pays back the debtor, to such a degree that he reserves no action to himself against him. But we are the sons of wrath, not only because we are corrupt, since we do not fulfill the law and do forbidden things, but also because it is necessary that we must appear pure before God, such as he created us. And we are not to be transgressors of the law, but even perfect doers of the law. Thus, so that we who would otherwise perish, might have full and perfect remission of all sins, it is necessary that this remission also match with the other remission concerning which we spoke before, which only removes one part of our sins. But we have found both in Christ whom we have apprehended by faith, who not only has suffered for our sins, but who also has fully sanctified our nature in himself for us, and fulfilled all righteousness for us, so that not only are we set free by him from death, but also we obtain the reward of eternal life in him.

Q168 Therefore, you conclude that in Christ alone, to whom we are joined by faith, is found all things necessary to us for salvation, so that in those who are in Christ, there is utterly no condemnation.

A168 I conclude so, and that this is the one knowledge of salvation.

Q169 You say also that this faith is a gift which is con-
ferred into us by the mere grace of God, and
therefore, that the beginning is from God, not
from us.

Acts 16:14
Eph. 2:8
Phil. 1:29

A169 I say so.

Q170 Now, please, let us ask to whom it is given. For
the thing itself witnesses to the fact that it is
not given to all, since the believers have always
been so few.

A170 But it does not follow, still, that it is not offered
to all. Therefore, it seems that we must first seek
whether it is offered to all; which question will
lead us to the source, namely, to providence and
predestination.

Q171 Let it be so, and therefore I ask, explain what
you mean by providence.

A171 I mean by it, not only that unspeakable power,
whereby it comes to pass that God has foreseen
all things from eternity, and most wisely
provided all things that were to be; but primar-
ily I mean by it that eternal decree of the most
wise and holy God, from whom anything that
has been, has been; and everything that is, is;
and everything that will be, will be, according
as it was pleasing to him to decree from eternity.

Q172 Therefore, do you say that this providence is
the effecter and moderator of all things?

A172 I say so, and to such a degree that it merits a
more excellent name than that of cause. For it
is that which orders all causes, and controls even
the smallest effects of them, so that they are carried to their decreed end.

Q173 But a part of the angels is evil, and all men are
evil by nature, and whatever proceeds from
them, must be evil (except regenerate men), as
that which proceeds from an evil beginning. But
God is not able to be the author of evil. Therefore, he is not the author of all things, if so
many evil things must be accepted.

A173 Both individual angels (for offspring is not able to be given in a spiritual nature) and the first people, Adam and Eve, were created good. Therefore, neither should be placed outside of the decree of God.

Q174 **So be it, in respect to that first or original state. But now since they are corrupt and depraved, how do you include them in the eternal decree of God which is so active and powerful, except that you involve God in the wickedness of them?**

A174 Certainly would it be equal, even by the judgement of demons or the most corrupt men, that they are exempt from the power of the creator God, since they are stiff-necked against him? Yet it must follow from what you say. However, so stands the case: Did you ever, I ask you, contemplate a clock, in which a certain very large wheel turning to the right, takes some others with it, some to the same right, but others to the left, with a completely contrary motion?

Q175 **Yes, and I often marveled that the industry of man is able to represent to my eyes, what man's mind is scarcely able to attain to in the orbs of the skies.**

A175 Know that this is a true image of that divine providence, if you except that to which nothing similar can be found, not even in the orbs of the skies, nor in mechanical instruments. For nothing is equal to or even like unto the Highest, namely, that God the omnipotent (whom now we have compared to the largest wheel which is the mover of the rest) is in such a way in the world, that He is not part of the world, and has given self-moving motion to each wheel moving itself; and in such a way that He Himself is moved by no means, and yet moves all things according to His own providence. Moreover, this *Eze. 1:5,etc.* mystery of the providence of God was represented to us in the vision of Ezekiel, in which we must observe this, that those four images were overcovered by wings, and the wheels infolded with wheels, with God placed highest above all things, lest we judge the mover to be moved with the causes, or lest too curiously we should hope to be able to perceive the reasons of those motions. With this posited, I respond to you threefold. First, instruments endowed with life and reason (such as angels and men) are led by God their maker in such a way, that they also lead themselves by their own inward, spontaneous motion, and therefore two causes run together to the causing of one action; namely, God who has separated himself from the instrument, and nevertheless grants to the instrument the very beginning of movement, and the instrument moving itself. Second, these instruments are moved by God in such a way, that he always leads well, but the instruments, if they are evil, lead with contrary motion, that is always evilly. But if the instrument is good, then only, since both the first author, who always moves well, and the instrument who moves itself, agree, does a good and praiseworthy action follow. Third, God moves evil instruments in such a way (for about these only do we now inquire), and these instruments, on the other hand, are so moved by themselves, that because of the twofold work which yet seems to be one, that in respect to the good beginning it is good, and in respect to the evil beginning it is bad.

Q176 I wish these things to be illustrated by examples.

A176 I will do it, even with sure and clear ones, when I have set forth this distinction. That God, the remarkable craftsman, using well whatever evil instruments there may be, does commit them against each other, or blesses the good by the work of them. Whichever he does, no one of sane mind denies that it is good, either to punish the evil, or benefit the good. Let us bring forth some examples. By the providence of God Joseph went down into Egypt, and was advanced into the greatest power so that he might be the preserver of the church. He himself said and declared these things. However, which instruments did God use in this matter? Satan, who impelled brothers against innocent brother, the evil will of the same brothers, the greed of the traders, and the lust of a very wicked woman. Therefore, they all deeply sinned, inasmuch as they were the beginning of their own actions. But God, using even these evil instruments who consider no such thing, was presiding for His own against famine, collected them in a fertile land, nurtured His faithful servant Joseph, and finally brought him to the highest degree of honor. Is it not a most righteous work of God, that the evil consume themselves? In this way He used the Midianites, using the spirit of discord, and the evil will of the murderers, when they made an attack one upon the other with evil intent, yet with right ful judgement of God. It was good that David was chastised, even after his sin was acknowledged and forgiven. It was even good that the treachery of Ahithophel and the wicked mind of Absalom lie open and be severely punished. The Lord used, to perform these things, the madness of Satan, the perfidy of Ahithophel, the very wicked ambition of Absalom, the abominable lust, and ungodliness, by which evil instruments God executes many things well. For he showed how such adultery and grief displeases him: He chastised David fatherly, he punished Ahithophel by his own hands, and finally he made Absalom destroy himself. Thus we are proven, and therefore are chastised by the good will of the heavenly Father, so that He might be glorified in this way; moreover, His power is

Gen. 45:7
and 50:20

Judg. 7:22

2 Sam. 12:22

2 Sam. 15:34
2 Sam. 17:14,23

2 Sam. 17:23
2 Sam. 18:9

1 Peter 3:17
1 Thes. 3:3,4
Gal. 6:14

perfected in our weakness, the Scripture testi-fies. And unless we are convinced of this, what comfort is there for the pious in so many miser-ies? But in the trial of Job the perversity of Satan is employed in this manner, and the greed and great cruelty of the robbers. Therefore, Satan sinned when he afflicted the servant of God with so many evils, and the robbers did wrong by stealing. However, God did right in testing His own servant, and in demonstrating that all attempts of Satan against the church are inef-fectual. Finally, you will not deny that the best of all the works of God is the redemption of mankind. For the Father delivered him up on account of our sins, by His own definite coun-sel, and by His prescribed eternal decree, as Peter and the church of Jerusalem said, and the Father is the one who did not spare His only Son for our sake. Yet, what instruments were employed to carry out such a thing? Yes, evil ones. For no good man is able to pursue, to prosecute, to damn, and to crucify an innocent man. But we all know that it was done by the spite of Satan entering into the heart of Judas, the great and detestable perfidy of Judas him-self, the jealousy and desperate improbity of the Jews, and by the softness and fickleness of Pilate. There is none of these who did not deeply sin, and for those sins everyone of them was afflicted by God with the most severe penalties. But we, meanwhile, by this same work, are saved from death and sin.

2 Cor. 12:9

Acts 2:23
Acts 4:28
Eph. 5:25
Rom. 8:39

Luke 22:3
John 12:6
Matt. 27:18

John 19:8

Q177 **But hence nothing else seems to be possible to gather, than that the counsels of the wicked are turned to contrary ends by God.**

A177 Yes, but more than that: evil men are also moved well and efficaciously by God, so that He might execute His own work through them. But you remember that which I said, namely, that evil men are moved well by God in such a way, to accomplish His own good work, not as the hammer or axe is in the hand of a craftsman, which are merely instruments, but in such a way that they also move themselves to do and will wrongly, since they are the active and powerful causes of their own evil works. Moreover, now it also must be added, that God works in the good and through the good, and through the evil, but not in the evil.

Q178 What difference is there in these terms?

A178 Actually, there is a great difference. For God uses as many good and bad instruments as He wants, and therefore, both through the good ones and the bad ones He is said to do His own work rightly. But God works in those only upon whom He breathes with His Holy Spirit, and over whom He rules, either confirming them in goodness, that is, angels and regenerate men; or endowing them with new goodness, as when He sanctifies His own first of all. But in the rest, He does not work within them by doing anything himself, but by giving them up to be moved and governed partly by their own desires, and partly by Satan: however, in such a way that their improbity may will and accomplish that which God himself rightfully ordained.

Rom. 8:14
1 Cor. 12:11
Eph. 1:11

John 14:17
Rom. 1:26,28
2 Tim. 2:26

Q179 Therefore, what do you think of the term "permission?"

A179 If by the word permission that difference is meant concerning which I just now spoke, that God does not work in evil people, but hands them over to Satan and to their own desires, I do not at all repudiate it. But if permission opposes will, I reject it, first as false, and second as utterly absurd. It is false because if God permits anything against His will, He is not God, that is, God almighty. But if He is said to permit something by not caring, how far are we from Epicureanism?[42] Therefore, it remains that willingly He permits what He permits. Thus, permission does not oppose will. Moreover, it is absurd, obviously, if it is false. But I say that this absurdity is able to be evident to any attentive person because of this: that the authors of this distinction whereby permission opposes will, do not only not attain to that which they wish (that is, that God not be considered the author of evil, which we confess to the utmost), but also they contradict utterly. For who is more at fault than He who sees an evil coming along ways ahead of time, and is able to impede it at will, but yet He not only does not impede it, but also He permits it, that is, He allows the power of that evil to come about? For not even those who think this way, do not deny that Satan, and even less evil men, may do anything evil except from prescription;like as someone who does not only not prohibit a fierce lion, which is locked in a cage, to hurt people, although He is easily able to, but also He loosens the chains, and would permit him to attack this man and that man. Perhaps you will say that the sins of men do merit this. I concede that. Nevertheless, it remains that the will of God agrees with His permission, just as when a magistrate delivers a criminal into the hand of the executioner, with the manner of his punishment supplied. And therefore it is absurd that will and permission are repugnant.

Q180 But then do evil people also do the will of God?
A180 If you understand will in its general signification, for that which God has willingly decreed to be, and you do not apply the term "doing" to the counsel of evil people, but to the outcome of the matter; clearly the Lord executes His will through evil men also, that is, because He decreed it from eternity. In accordance with that, who will resist the will of God? But if by the term "will" you mean that which is pleasing to God

Rom. 9:19

Psalm 5:5

Mark 3:35

in and of itself, and by the term "doing" you include the proper state of obedience, then respond plainly, that evil men not only do not do the will of God, but also they do contrary to it.

Q181 I did not get an answer. Nevertheless, I return to that which you responded, that all things were created good by God in the beginning. From whence then is the fault? For if fault enters aside from the decree of God, what you have said falls, that nothing is utterly exempt from the active and powerful providence of God. But if the decree of God precedes, how is He Himself (which is said apart from blasphemy) not the author of all evil?

A181 The cause of fault is the very spontaneous inclination of the will of good angels and the first humans to evil. For the Lord created them changeably good, since to be immutably good *per se* belongs to God alone.

Q182 Therefore, both the angels who have never fallen and never will fall, and everyone who will be gathered into eternal life, are gods.

A182 I deny the consequence. For that the blessed angels never have fallen or will fall, and that there will be no end of eternal bliss, is not from immutable nature, which is proper to God alone, but because they are perpetually sustained by the power of the immutable God; whereby, if perchance He should desert them (moreover, God would desert them, if He wished), then clearly not only would they be able to be changed, they would utterly evaporate and be reduced to nothing. Therefore, I say that the cause of the fault is the spontaneous inclination of the will, created good, but changeable. For that will was changeable, by God who created it that way. For otherwise, as many unchangeable natures He made, so many gods He made. And it was changed by God deserting it (for to whom is He bound?), but changing itself willingly, so that the cause of the fault seems to stand from defect rather than effect.

Q183 **But if this change does not take place apart from the decreed will of God, clearly it seems that all this evil must be attributed to Him.**

A183 Not at all does it follow, since the decree of God does not take away the will of man, and thus his deliberation or choosing, but only orders it. For he was changed by falling entirely spontaneously, which must be understood much more in regard to the fall of angels, into whom the blame itself crept from at home, which was the reason perhaps that moved God to pity man, who fell at the intervention of the devil, and not to have pity upon the devil and his angels.

Q184 **But otherwise it is not able to come to pass, except God decreed it.**

A184 I concede both. For it is not right to exclude the eternal decree from the changing of the first work[43] - that decree wherein a little before we showed that one and all, without any exception, are comprehended. And to declare that a decree of this type is changeable, is impious. Therefore, let both be most true. But from thence it does not follow, either that God, who always does well, is at fault, just as we have said, whenever the instruments should sin; or that man is outside of fault, as he who sinned willingly. For this necessity, whereby what God decreed must come to pass, did not take away either will or contingency, but rather ordered them, since among the causes of man's actions the chief is the will.

Q185 **Therefore, you mean that the necessity of choosing what God decreed from eternity strives not against His will. But contingency is that which may or may not happen.**

A185 I say even more openly, that will or contingency

are not removed by necessity, but by compulsion. It was necessary that Christ die in the age, time, and place ordained from eternity, or otherwise the prophets might have lied. But if you consider the natural disposition of the flesh of Christ in and of itself, outside of the divine decree, there is no doubt but that naturally he would have been able to live longer, and therefore that in this respect he would have died contingently. The bones of Christ might have been broken, if you only view the nature of bones themselves. But if you view the decree of God, they were no more able to be broken than the opinion of God is able to change. Thus, the unchangeable necessity of the divine decree, does not remove the contingency of the second cause, but disposes it. Also, Christ died necessarily from the decree of the Father, and yet He did so willingly. And God forbid that we should ever die unwillingly, yet it is ordained that we die once. What more? God Himself is most freely and greatly willing, yet unchangeably good. Therefore, will and necessity are not repugnant. For since it was necessary that only one of two repugnant things be chosen by Adam, although neither was determined within his will, still one was definite in the eternal decree of God, which was outside and above Adam's will, yet did not compel his will: but it willingly and spontaneously, since it could not take both, inclined finally to that part which the decree of God had established.

Matt. 26:54-56

John 13:11,18

John 19:36

Acts 17:3

Q186 **But certainly that necessity, which together with lust entered the heart of man, in such a manner that he could not help but sin (just as you declared before), seems to remove contingency.**

A186 Although I should confess it to be so, still men cannot be exempted from blame. First, because this necessity of sinning, with which the human race is now oppressed, is not from the Creator, but from the spontaneous (as we have said) inclination of man's natural will to evil. Moreover, who would marvel that he is burned, who hurls himself willingly into a fire? Again, although man is not now carried to evil contingently or by chance, but out of utter necessity, since after the corruption of sin (as the Apostle said) he is enslaved to sin, until freed by the Son of God. Yet that which he does, he does spontaneously, and not from coercion. For just as he cannot help but do evil, so also he delights in nothing other than evil, while the evil, now and then lurking under the guise of good, deceives him. And therefore, not even this necessity, which was brought in through the spontaneous fall, does remove the spontaneous moving of the will. With that granted, it follows that man is the cause of sin, since, although he sins necessarily, he also sins willingly. But still I do not even say that contingency is removed by this necessity. For although in a man who is bound under the necessity of sin, and is not yet regenerated, there now remains no deliberation either to choose the true good, or evil, as was in human nature before the Fall; still there remains a deliberating between this or that evil. For where there is no choice concerning this or that, there is no deliberation. But even the most wicked men deliberate. But they can neither understand something, nor think anything, and therefore much less deliberate concerning something, except they either wander away from the good, or else against their conscience. Therefore, all the deliberation of them is turned to choice between two or more evils. Moreover, that they prefer the one or the other, it also happens altogether contingently, in respect to their own spontaneous will, which contingency the immutable decree of God now no more removes, than it did long ago in the uncorrupted man.

Rom. 7:14

John 8:36

Rom. 8:7

Q187 **Therefore, the sum of these things which you have said concerning providence, is this: Noth-**

ing at all happens without God's will or knowledge (that is, by chance or accident), but totally as God himself decreed it from eternity, disposing all the intermediate causes powerfully and efficaciously, so that they are necessarily brought to their destined end, in respect to His decree. Nevertheless, He is not the author or allower of any evil, since He always acts most righteously, with whatever instruments He executes His works.

A187 It is so.

Q188 This is still the thing which bothers me. For although I see that God works rightly through evil men, nevertheless, if each and every thing comes to pass by the eternal decree of God, in such a way that nothing is excluded, it remains, that the evil works of the evil, are not exempt from the decree of God, which seems to me cannot be said without impiety.

A188 It is necessary that He be vehemently troubled and frustrated, who labors in order to comprehend the wisdom of God within the bounds of his own wisdom. For, please, if you should want to include the ocean in a drinking cup, what else could you do but fail, and be rightly held as insane? But more tolerable, although not to be spoken of, is the proportion between the ocean and the smallest cup, than between the wisdom of God, and the foolishness of man's very corrupt mind. Nevertheless, I think that what you object can be responded to well enough. Thus, I grant you even this, that the evil works of the evil, even as they are evil in respect to themselves, are not done apart from God's will or knowledge, since, if that were so, Atheism and Epicureanism would follow; but I add, if you have in view the decree of God, the evil itself has a bit of good, although it is evil in and of itself, so that this paradox of Augustine is most true; that since there is good, there are evils, although God did not allow there to be evils. Moreover, He does not permit unwillingly, but willingly.

Q189 What then? Shall we say that God wishes iniquity?

A189 May it never be. For to say so is the most horrible of all blasphemies. But control yourself a little while, please, while I expound upon that which I have said so truly and piously, so it cannot be denied, except God is avouched not to be the judge of this world. The term "will" is sometimes broadly taken for that which God ordained, by which signification we must wholly say, that either God wills all things (that is, that nothing happens which God does not want to happen), or that God is not omnipotent (since something happens, however small, which God does not want to happen), or that God does not care for all things (since things happen from His neglect). But sometimes, by the term 'will," only that which pleases Him is meant, because it is good by its own nature. After this manner, only the good are said to obey God, and to follow His will; because in this sense God is only said to will, that is, to approve and to hold as pleasing, that which is good, and not to will iniquity; which will He fully revealed to us in the Law; but the other will is not the same, but in part. For who knows anything that will happen, even on this very day? For nothing happens except that which God willed and decreed from eternity to happen.

Psalms 5:4

Q190 But can God be thought to will anything which he does not approve, and thus that which is evil?

A190 Truly, it must be confessed, that whatever God decreed, it is ordained altogether willingly, but here also shines forth His infinite wisdom, that with Him even the darkness has a bit of light, yet in such a way that it is and remains darkness, that is, it is good also that there should be evil; for God found the method whereby it might happen, that what is and remains evil by its own nature, might still have a bit of good before Him, and (as Augustine rightly and elegantly said) it may not happen except by His will, that is, apart from His decree, and yet be against His will, that is, what is by its own nature unrighteous, and therefore does not please God. For example, that God saved His own by the gracious redemption of His own Son Christ, is to His own exceedingly great glory, which otherwise would not have shone forth. But man would not have required redemption from sin and death, unless sin and death existed. Therefore, in respect to the ordinance of God, it was good that sin and death enter into the world; and yet this sin is and remains sin so much by its own nature, that it could not be expiated for except by a very terrible penalty. Again, we receive far more in Christ, than we lost in Adam. Therefore, it was best and most useful for us that Adam fell, in respect to God, who prepares a kingdom of eternal glory for us by this wonderful means. And nevertheless, this Fall is so evil by its own nature, that even those who are justified and believe, experience many miseries and calamities from it, even to death. Also, this is the great glory of God, that He shows Himself to be a most severe punisher of sin. But if sin had not existed, no opening would be made for this judgement. Therefore, it was good, in respect to the ordinance of God, that sin exist, and afterwards be spread abroad, which is damned in the demons and all those who are outside of Christ, with eternal punishment. Likewise, this also is the will of God (Peter said), that is, His decree, that all who do right, are affected by evils. But he who does well, is not able to be hurt apart from sin. It is good therefore, in respect to God's will (that is, His ordinance) that there be perse-

Rom. 5:15

1 Peter 3:17

cutors of the church, whom, notwithstanding, He most severely punishes, justly, as sinners against His will, that is, against that which He approves of them doing. Therefore, by the express words of the apostles, that which is against God's will or decree (that is, against that which He approves and commands), does not come to pass; on the other hand, it cannot be said that God is contrary to Himself, or that He wills iniquity, as Augustine rightly concluded from the Word of God against Julian.[44]

Q191 Therefore, it seems right that permission be distinguished from will.

A191 What should be thought concerning this distinction I addressed a little before. Certainly, if permission is set against will, that is decree, this opposition is not only false, but is also foolish and ridiculous. Even if in those actions which are not of free choice in and of themselves, as when merchants who are in danger throw their goods overboard, and generally as often as men choose the lesser evil to avoid the greater inconvenience, even profane men know that free will has dominion. But if you set permission against will, that is, to that which God wants, as pleasing and acceptable to Him in and of itself, and by its own nature; so that that which is good in and of itself is matched with that which is good by chance, and like as from the immense wisdom of God the darkness all serves the purpose of light, it has some measure of good (clearly, not by its own nature, but in respect to its end to which it is guided by God), then I would admit it; only this should be added, that this permission is not vain and idle, as some sleep, but very active and powerful, and yet most righteous permission, which can best be understood in a few words. I don't think that you would say that a judge is a certain idle spectator, when he hands criminals over to the executioner after hearing his case to receive this or that kind of punishment. For the executioner doesn't put him to death so much as he is the instrument of the judge who puts him to death. So if anything happens cruelly from the sentence of the judge, it is attributed, not so much to the executioner who executes, as to the judge who commands.

Q192 **I concede all these things. But how many dissimilarities are there between these illustrations and the things which we are discussing!**

A192 I confess. For otherwise there is no, or at least very little difference between a like thing and a same thing. Nevertheless, I wish that the chief points be brought up by you, so I can respond to them individually.

Q193 **In the sentencing of judges, a trial goes before; but in these things concerning which you entreat, often nothing of this trial is observed.**

A193 How many things are done rightly by the magistrates of this world, whose trial does not appear to the subjects. And do you attribute less to God, who searches thoroughly all things past and future lying hid in the depth of the hearts of men?

Q194 **The executer does nothing except from sentences received. But where have evil men received any such command as to kill one another, or to harm good men?**

A194 In this you are deceived, that whatever God decreed, you think that He gives knowledge of it with some loud voice, to those whose works He has decreed to use. However, experience has shown this is not always true in either case, that is, whether He has decided to use mercy, or to use justice, not even when He uses knowing instruments. For who would doubt that Pharaoh was ordained by God to receive Joseph and to prepare a hospitable place for the Church? Yet he himself outwardly received no mandate concerning this, no, nor even thought of any such thing in himself. Yet this was decreed by God, and the quiet motion of Pharaoh's heart tended to the executing of that which the Lord decreed. The prophets predicted a thousand times that the Chaldeans were ordained to punish the evil Israelites, and to nurture the good; and in the same way, as if Nebuchadnezar had received an express mandate concerning this, so the Lord did not expressly command any such thing to the Chaldeans, but, as Ezekiel wrote, the heart of the king, partly given to Satan and his seers, and partly to his own desires, willingly inclined him to accomplish that which God had determined. How much more must the same be believed, as often as the Lord uses the things which lack reason, or even that which is utterly without life, as his executioners. For in this way He called flies, frogs, locusts, grasshoppers, hail, and death to punish Pharaoh; so also the wisest of all men said, that even lots themselves do not fall by chance. For by a secret motion all things serve the executing of the decrees of God. But there is this difference, that good instruments do nothing except by faith, that is, upon assurance that they are called to do that which they do, and with a mind fixed to obey. But as for the evil instruments, since they are led with a blind force by Satan and their own lusts, and have not the least consideration for obedience to God, with whose express word they know, or ought to know, that their counsels strive. Therefore, they do not serve the Lord, although God secretly uses the work of them, even the unwilling, so that they do nothing else, than that which He Himself, the wonderful worker, has decreed.

Gen. 45:2
Psalm 105:17

Jer. 25:9

Eze. 21:21

Exo. 7:18
Prov. 16:33

Q195 **Therefore, let us speak concerning God's providence no further, from which I see absolutely nothing can be exempted. Thus, let us (if you**

please) proceed to predestination, which I wish you to describe to me at the outset.

A195 Predestination, considered in general, is nothing else than that very thing which we call the decree of God, but with regard to the end and scope of the decree. For there is nothing which the most wise creator of all things (who neither made anything rashly, nor is able to be deceived or change His counsel) has not decreed both to middle ends, and especially to some ultimate scope. But common belief is that predestination is seen chiefly in the governing of human kind. Therefore, we will describe it this way: we say that it is the eternal and immutable decree of God, going in order before all the causes of salvation and damnation, whereby God has determined to be glorified in some by saving them in Christ by mere grace, but in others by damning them by His rightful judgement in Adam and in themselves. From the use of Scripture we call the former vessels of glory, and elect, that is, predestined to salvation from eternity through mercy; the latter are called reprobates and vessels of wrath, that is, those who are predestined likewise to rightful damnation from eternity (both of which God knew individually from eternity).

Q196 **But it is hard to say that some are predestined to death, and therefore you know that many apply the term "predestination" only to the elect, and that the reprobates are instead foreknown.**

A196 I know what this means. Some were afraid lest they make God the cause of the destruction of the reprobates, and also imply that He is cruel, if they confess that the reprobates are predestined by God; but neither option needed to be feared, as we will show in its due place. For if foreknowledge (as they call it) has the force of cause no less than predestination, they say the very thing which they do not wish to say. But if it does not have the force of cause, then come, let them say also that God is not the cause of the salvation of the predestined. For the Apostle, while enumerating the cause of the salvation of the elect, set down "prognosis" (which they interpret as foreknowledge) in the first place. And Luke also set down "prognosis" as the ground of our redemption. Therefore, Augustine, although now and then he distinguished predestination from foreknowledge, nevertheless rightly acknowledged both as predestination.[45] But let this strife of terms be away! I only wished to show that I had rightly made predestination a general term, whereof there are two sorts, which still run together in the end no less (it must especially be observed), than in the beginning and origin. For the head of them both is the decree of God. But both the ways (which are, as it were, divided from this head) run together again in the extreme end; namely, in the glory of God. With these things posited, that I might respond to that exception of yours, that it seems a hard matter that some are predestined to death, I say that the following seems much harder to me: namely, that God did not set forth for Himself a certain end in creating men, although (as the unwisest workmen does rightly testify) the end is the first intention of the doer. That God did set forth for Himself an end in creating men that fell into uncertainty, in such a way that it rests in the power of the clay, and not in the power of the potter, to make either that happen, or not happen, which was purposed by the worker. That God, knowing the will of His own handiwork, changed His purpose, so that although He decreed all to be saved in Christ, nevertheless, those who did not wish to incline themselves to this purpose, were destroyed after He changed His mind. For all these things I say necessarily

Rom. 8:29
Acts 2:23

are consequences of their doctrines, who believe that those who perish, do so contrary to the predestination of God. And lest we seem to wander outside of our bounds, that is, to employ only arguments of consequence, first I say that all doctrines which strive against the analogy of faith (of which type this must be, which, when granted, so many wicked things follow) are shattered by the Scriptures. Then I say, that as often as the Scriptures make mention of the predestination of the elect - so often is the predestination of the reprobate confirmed, when the matter itself requires that, whereas some are elected to life, the rest must be understood to be predestined to death. Furthermore, if the vessels of glory are said to be predestined to glory, the opposition of contradictions wholly requires, that we should consider the vessels of wrath as predestined to death.

Rom. 9:22-23

Q197 **But here it is noted, that when he deals with the vessels of glory, the Apostle uses a word which indicates doing, and when he deals with the vessels of wrath, he uses a passive participle.**

A197 I concede that if it is concerned with middle causes, whereby the vessels of wrath are carried to the wrath predestined for them, they themselves are the only cause of their own destruction. But this distinction is clearly futile. For Luke, when writing concerning the elect, uses the passive participle "having been ordained to eternal life." But what? Was that of themselves, and not rather from the mere grace of God? It is no matter. For we are not concerned with salvation or damnation, but with the decree of salvation or damnation, which disposes the very causes of the execution, yet so that it does not hang from them, "For that is utterly up the river," as the old proverb says.[46] Finally, is it harder to say that some are predestined to

Acts 13:48

destruction, than to say that they are ordained to damnation long ago, as Jude says, or to say they are appointed to wrath, as Paul says? Lastly, I did not say that their destruction is the end set forth by the decree of God, but His glory. Nor did I simply say, that they are predestined to destruction, but that they are predestined to a just destruction; meaning that although no one is condemned except he whom the Lord predestined to condemnation (otherwise, those blasphemies about which I formerly spoke would necessarily follow), still no one is condemned except he who is found to have in himself just causes for condemnation. Then what falseness or harshness does our former point have?

Jude 4

1 Thess. 5:9

Q198 **You seem to be refuted by this saying: that God wills all men to be saved, and by like universal passages.**

1 Tim. 2:4

A198 Therefore, say that some are damned by an unwilling God, or confess that the said text must be understood otherwise, which the promises also show; namely, in such a way that (which the Scholastics themselves also saw) not each individual of kinds is understood, but kinds of individuals. And (as I would say more plainly) it is not a universal proposition, but an indefinite one, which instead ought to be translated, "God wishes any manner of men to be saved." Matthew uses the same kind of speech when he says that all (that is, all sorts of) sicknesses and diseases were healed by the Lord, as Latinists now and then speak. For please, who dares to say that God wishes all men to be saved, even those who continue in unbelief to the very end? No, certainly not. For if this is the will of the Father, that he who believes in the Son should not perish, it follows that this is also His will, that those who do not believe in the Son, perish. And therefore, those two things, namely, to be saved

Matt. 4:23

John 6:40

and to come to a knowledge of the truth, must be yoked, so that it might be understood, that God only wishes those to be saved whom He wishes to come to an acknowledgement of the truth. But faith (which is this true knowledge), is neither of all men, as the apostle testifies, nor is it by running or willing, but by the mercy of God; but it is of those only who (as Luke said) are ordained to eternal life, and whose heart (as Luke also said) God opened to attend the word of God. Therefore, let us understand that the predestination of God extends to all sorts of men, that is, both Jews and Gentiles, private persons and magistrates, men and women, young and old, slaves and gentlemen, both great sinners and lesser sinners. For these only and the like of the same circumstances, are those things which are included in the former passage.

Eph. 1:8
2 Thess. 2:3
Rom. 9:16
Acts 13:48
Acts 16:14

Q199 Therefore, you wish to make election particular?

A199 But I ask whether any sane man could imagine a universal election? For certainly he who receives all, elects none. And he who elects anything from two or more, must necessarily be said to repudiate those things which he does not elect.

Q200 But certainly the calling and promise are universal.

A200 Understand them to be indefinite (and indeed, in respect to the certain circumstances about which I spoke) and you will think more correctly. And in this way those things must wholly be accepted, which some very learned men of our time have written about this controversy. For otherwise, see how that universal calling is refuted by necessary reasons. For if by calling you mean the preaching of the Word, it is false that all men are or ever will be called individually in this manner. For how many have died, are dying, or will die, before they have heard any bit of this Word? But if you mean that other,

Rom. 1:19 much broader calling, namely, that contemplation of nature, from which a knowledge of God is understood, even this is not so universal, that it comprehends every individual without exception. For how many have died and daily do die in that age which is utterly unfit for that contemplation? Therefore, neither calling or any election can or ought to be considered universal, but only indefinite (and only with those certain circumstances, I mentioned, excluded).

Q201 **But what if we say that all men are called universally to salvation under a condition, if they believe. And therefore, in respect to God who calls, the salvation is offered universally; moreover, that this calling is not universally efficacious, is not from God's doing, but from the stubbornness of unbelievers who refuse the good gift offered them?**

A201 This is doubtless true in some respect. For there is no doubt but that the stubbornness of the unbelievers is that which impedes the application and efficacy of the promises which are offered. There is also no doubt but that calling *Matt. 20:1-16* is broader in scope than election. But still, those things are neither said truly or fitly enough. For first we have shown, that not even the outward calling (whether you view that which is natural, or that which is done by the Word of the Gospel) pertains to every individual person. Therefore, in those about whom we speak, there is found no stubbornness against the offered Gospel, but only original corruption, which still, even by itself, is sufficient to condemn the reprobates. Furthermore, although the condition of believing is joined to it, yet the decree does not hang from it, but instead the condition hangs upon the decree, as that which proceeds all inferior causes. Otherwise, see how false and absurd are the consequences. For it would follow that God, in deliberating, first set before Himself the work as if it were already completed, and according as He foresaw it to be affected by itself, and not by its Creator, from that He took occasion to decree, that is, to either predestine to salvation or death. Or even if it is best to you that it was uncertain how the fulfilling or not fulfilling of the event would happen, it has to be concluded, that the decree of God hangs in suspense, and the judgement (as Augustine elegantly said) is not in hands of the potter, but in the power of the clay. And hereupon another very false doctrine will be grounded, namely, that the beginning of faith is not from God, but from the will of man, if God's foresight has given cause to the decree of election. Nor is it what you may object, that faith is not forseen, inasmuch as it is a gift of God which comes from the outside; but rather corruption and unbelief are forseen, which are natural in men after the Fall. For the law of contraries requires in every case, that in whatever step faith is placed in the decree of election, in the same place unbelief must be set in the decree of reprobation. Therefore, if you make foreknown faith as the cause of the decree of election (which is merely Pelagianism,[47] and therefore was repealed by Augustine) it is necessary that you deem the same in the contrary decree of reprobation. And again, if you subordinate faith to that decree (as it entirely must be done, for we are elected to believe, not because we believe), in the contrary member it is necessary that you subordinate unbelief to the decree of reprobation.

Q202 **But will you make the decree of election as the cause of faith, as also you make the decree of reprobation to be the cause of unfaithfulness.**

A202 No. For that decree is truly the efficient cause of faith. But corruption or unbelief with its fruits is subordinated to the decree in such a way, that still the will of man is the first efficient cause of them, and yet they are subject to the decree, since although it is not through the decree, yet it is not apart from or besides the decree, that those things happen, whose (as I have said) deficient cause, but not the efficient cause, rests in God. For just as they only believe, in whom God created faith, so by God forsaking the will of men, sin comes into mankind, and remains and bears fruit in as many as it pleases God to give up to their own lusts, so that they are the causes of their own destruction, to which also they are registered and predestined from eternity. Furthermore, so that I may return to that other question, whatever is said about that condition attached to the decree, as if the decree itself depends upon that condition, it is unfitly said. For the decree to save the elect is different than the very glorification of the elect. And the decree of damning the wicked is different than the damnation of the wicked, since the decree must be distinguished from its execution. Therefore, the execution of the decree of election depends upon apprehending Christ by faith. And the execution of reprobation (the damnation of the wicked) depends upon sin and its fruits, just like that saying of the prophet, "your destruction, Israel, is from yourself." Moreover, of the decree of electing certain men to be saved by grace, and certain men to be condemned on account of their sins, we know no other cause but this one, that the Lord who is of the highest mercy and justice, in this way wishes to be glorified. He who does not acquiesce in this,since he seeks something higher and more just than the will of God, he is rightfully reproved by the apostle as a babbler.

Joel 13:9

Q203 **Therefore God hates some, not on account of their sin, but because it pleases him to do so.**

A203 This is a calumnious objection. For it is certain that no one is despised of God except for sin, for otherwise He would be hating His own work. But it is one thing to hate, and another to predestine to just hatred. For the cause of that hatred is clear, that is, sin. But why God predestined those whom he wished to just hatred, even though the cause is hidden to us (except the end of His glory), nevertheless, it cannot be called unrighteous, since the will of God is the only rule of righteousness. For if we speak concerning the supreme will of God which orders the causes of all things, we must not say that anything is righteous before God wills it. But on the other hand, God must will something before it is right; whoever does not consider that, will have reasoned confusedly on this matter.

Q204 **But still God seems to be a regarder of persons if he does not attribute equal things to equals. In this all men are equal, that they are corrupted by nature propagated by the one Adam.**

A204 No, it does not follow that whoever does not attribute equal things to equal people is a respecter of persons, but only he who does not attribute equal to equal, since he is moved by certain circumstances inherent in the persons themselves: as if a judge should acquit one of two equal offenders because he is rich, or a friend, or a countryman. For these are the persons who must not be regarded by the one who would judge uncorruptly. But let us place two men indebted to you for the same amount under the same conditions. If you forgive liberally one of your debtors, and exact from the other the full amount, was there any regarding of persons here? What if some sovereign, with two like offenders before him, forgives the sin of one by mere grace, and afflicts the other with rightful penalties, was there any regarding of persons here? No, for if there is any wrong in this kind of dealing, certainly it is not in him to whom punishment was given, but in him rather to whom pardon was made, and he will seem to be wronged by a remission of blame. Therefore, in this argument which we are now discussing, much less can any respecter of persons be considered, since God does not acquit the elect except by the imputed satisfaction of Christ; and if anything here is able to be called into inquiry as having been done less than justly, it seems that men must doubt rather concerning the mercy to the elect than concerning the just severity to the wicked. Finally, for what purpose are all these things? For in the order of causes God's decree goes before the very creation of mankind, unless you want to say that God was so foolish a workman, that he created mankind before He decided in Himself for what purpose He would create them. Moreover, what could He contemplate in those who did not yet exist, whereby He might be moved to determine this or that concerning them? Therefore, this discourse also pertains not to decree, but to the execution of the decree, in which (as I have already said) still no partiality can be found.

Q205 **Therefore, do you not understand by the term "lump" used by the apostle as the created and corrupted mankind, from which God predestined some to honor and others to dishonor?**

Rom. 9:21

A205 There is no doubt but that God takes both from the same corrupt lump, and predestines them to different ends. Nevertheless, I say and utterly affirm, that Paul in that similitude rises also to that highest decree to which even the very creation of mankind is subordinated in the order of causes, and the apostle does not even place His foreknowledge of man's corruption before it. For first by the term "lump" there is clearly signified a material still unshaped, and only prepared for a future work. Again, comparing God to a potter, and mankind to a lump of clay from which vessels are later to be make, the apostle without a doubt means the first creation of men. Furthermore, it is unproper to say that vessels of wrath are made from this lump. For already they are vessels of dishonor, if this means corrupt men, and the potter should not be said to make them, other than such as they had already made themselves. Finally, no less should the cause of the decree of reprobation be manifest than the cause of the decree of execution, that is, the cause of the damnation of the reprobates. The cause is corruption. But why then did the apostle rise up to that secret will of God, which is to be honored rather than scrutinized, although he had a ready response, and which had a probability even to human reason?

Q206 **Indeed, you compel me to assent to you even in this point. But something else is bothering me. If this decree is necessary and unchangeable, as clearly it is, for what purpose do men weary themselves? For whether they do well, if they are predestined to destruction, they must necessarily perish. Or should they do evilly, if they are predestined to life, they will be saved.**

A206 Clearly, it is a ridiculous objection, which presupposes that which cannot, nor ever will come to pass. For whence is repentance and its fruits? Certainly from the regenerating Spirit of Christ, apprehended through faith. But that true faith is only given to the elect. Therefore, only the elect repent, and pursue good works. The rest do not wish to think anything rightly, and much less to do it, since to will and do right, which is peculiar only to the elect, also comes from the grace of God. Therefore, also vain is the saying of them who say that they will be saved, if they are elect, no matter to what life they give themselves. For as many as are elect, they are the sons of God. But if they are the sons *Rom. 8:14* of God, the apostle said, then they are led by the Spirit of God. Thus the elect are not able to perish (for either God's decree would fail, or certainly God would be mutable). But just as they are not able to perish, so in their own time they

are endowed with faith, ingrafted into Christ,
in whom they, having been justified and sanctified, are finally glorified.

Q207 **But yet it is necessary that those who are predestined to destruction perish.**

A207 I concede; but because they are sinners. For
always between the decree and execution of it
there intervenes sin, which will shut up the
mouths of any men who are full of complaints.
For what is more right than that God punishes
sins? And to whom is mercy due? Therefore, I
am not accustomed to marveling that any perish, but rather that God could be so good, that
all do not perish.

Q208 **Since you have so often distinguished middle
causes from the decrees that order them, I wish
that you also would review them from each
side.**

A208 Since God had decreed from eternity (as can be
perceived from the events) to reveal His glory
the most in mankind, which rests partly in excer-
cising mercy, and partly in demonstrating His
hatred of sin, He created man whole from within
and without, and endowed him with right
understanding and will, but mutable. For He
Himself, being the highest good, cannot create
or will any evil. Yet, unless evil had entered into
the world, there would be no room for mercy
or justice. Therefore man, being mutable, enslaved himself and all his descendants to sin and
to the wrath of God, willingly and merely contingently, in respect to the beginning inherent
in man himself, that is, his will, although it was
necessary if you have in view the decree and
working out of the matter. From thenceforth the
Lord (according as He had determined from eternity) bringing forth some now and then, does
so lead them to their appointed ends to be glorified in them on either side, that those in whose
salvation He wishes to reveal His own glory, He

Rom. 8:28

Rom. 11:35

Rom. 9:22

transfers some immediately to eternal life who are freely comprehended in His covenant, and others, if He wishes them to live longer, are called by the effectual Word of the Gospel, sometimes earlier, sometimes later, and grafts them in Christ, in whom He justifies and sanctifies them, and gives them eternal life. But as for the others who are predestined to His own rightful vengeance (for to whom is He a debtor?), either He destroys them immediately, or patiently watching over them, so that they might not be utterly inexperienced of His goodness, either He does not call them at all, or inasmuch as He calls them, they are more inexcusable. From whence it happens that they, having been left to their own lusts, harden themselves, until the measure of their iniquity is complete, and they pass to judgement. And how these causes of the destruction of the reprobates in such a way come to pass, so that, besides the decree of God, who forsakes the reprobates and delivers them to Satan and to themselves, the whole blame for the evil in them is their responsibility, we have shown in its own place.

Q209 Therefore, the vessels of mercy should praise the Lord, and the vessels of wrath condemn themselves. But in the perilous temptation of particular election, where should I flee for succor?

A209 To the effects whereby the spiritual life is rightly discerned, and likewise our election, just as the life of the body is perceived from its feeling and moving. For we who wallow in the mudhole of this world, are not able to raise ourselves to that highest light unless we climb by those steps whereby God draws His elect to himself according to His eternal decree, as those whom He created to His own glory. Therefore, that I am elect, is first perceived from sanctification begun in me, that is, by my hating of sin and my lov-

Phil. 2:13

1 John 3:10
Rom. 8:15,16

Psalms 42:11

ing of righteousness. To this I will add the testimony of the Spirit, comforting my conscience as David said: "Why are thou cast down, O my soul? And why art thou disquieted within me? Hope thou in God; for I shall yet praise him, who is the health of my countenance, and my God." Hereto pertains the serious minding of God's benefits, which, although it rather terrifies us than consoles us while we think on our own thanklessness, nevertheless, in the end it must uplift us, since always in it is seen the manifest signs of His free and unchangeable fatherly love towards us, not shadowed, but openly expressed. From this sanctification and comfort of the Spirit we gather faith. And therefore we rise to Christ, to whom whosoever is given, is necessarily elect from all eternity in Him, and will never be ejected from the doors.

Q210 What if those testimonies are faint?
A210 Then we know that we are tried, and therefore, that our sluggishness is greatly to be blamed. Yet still our minds must not be despondent, but must be strengthened by those indefinite promises, and again throw darts at our adversary. For although the struggle of our flesh against our spirit (especially as often as the Spirit seems to fall apart and be quenched) does bring great doubts to our consciences concerning the truth of our faith, still it is certain that this spirit which truly (although faintly) opposes the assaults of the flesh, is the spirit of adoption, whose gift is not to be repented of. For otherwise, the elect would be able to perish, and those who were justified might fall from Christ. From this it would follow that either God is mutable, or that the falling out of His decree is uncertain, neither of which can be attributed to God without blasphemy.

Q211 But the crown is given only to those who persevere.

A211 I concede, and therefore, whoever is elect seeks perseverance and obtains it.

Q212 Then do you think that the Spirit of adoption is never shaken?

A212 I confess that the Spirit is now and then interrupted in severe temptations, and that the testimonies of Him who dwell in us are so made unconscious, that for a time He seems to be utterly departed from us. Nevertheless, I say that He is never taken away, since the decree of God to save His own must be firm, and therefore, at the right time, finally the clouds of the flesh are chased away, and the happiness of the salvation of the Lord always returns, and shines as the sun into the troubled consciences of the elect. Finally, I say that true faith and its effects are interrupted in the elect like in those whose faculties of the mind are impeded by a sleeping disease or as in drunkmen; still their minds are not removed, since there is a great difference between a sleeping disease and drunkenness, and death. But those who have the Spirit of adoption have a sure pledge of eternal life. Therefore, in this most perilous struggle, the very thing by which Satan assaults us, can and must hold forth certain victory to us. For unless the Spirit of adoption (who also is the Spirit of sanctification, justification, life, and faith) is present in us, there would be no struggle, and the reign of sin would be peaceful in us. For this is what the man who does not have that Spirit within him says: "I do the evil I want to do. I do not do good, nor do I want to." But those who are regenerate and elect, who are still struggling, say, "I do the evil which I do not want to do, and I do not do the good I want to do. Woe is me. Who will free me from the body of this death?" And while crying out these things, the elect person casts his anger on the very throne of God the Father, whom he beheld

Rom. 7:13

Rom. 7:15

Rom. 7:25

in the preaching of the Word and in the sacraments. Finally, the elect who have already taken hold of the full glory in the other world, say this: "I do the good I want to do, and I do not do the evil I do not wish to do."

Q213 What if a man never senses the testimonies of the Spirit within himself?

A213 Still it must not be established that he is one of the number of the reprobates. For the Lord calls His own at the time that pleases Him. Therefore, such men must be sent away to the Word and sacraments, where they may hear God speaking, calling sinners to Himself. For although they do not participate in the fruit or effects of them for a time, still they must encourage themselves and also be diligently incited by others, to persevere in the hearing of God's voice even against their will, and then at some time to obtain what the Lord defers, not to cast them away, but on the contrary, to sharpen their desire and solicitude.

Q214 Therefore, I would wish to discuss the sacraments also, about which there is especially such contention in the Church today.

A214 Indeed I do not refuse this. Nevertheless (I hope) it will be done more conveniently at another time.[48] Meanwhile, if you are satisfied with my answers to your questions, I am very glad, and I hope that you will seriously meditate on these things day and night.

FINIS

NOTES

1. "Singularis bonitas" [5] a goodness alone of its kind. As both Augustine and Aquinas put it, God is *"summum bonum."*
2. This answer is very similar to the answer given to question 4 of the Westminster Larger Catechism.
3. This formula was hammered out in the Council of Nicea in an effort to uphold the ontological connection of the Father and Son.
4. In other words, for every person there is one man. Since there are three persons in the Godhead, are there three Gods?
5. God is simple in that He is free from any composition or division into parts, and thus the three persons are not segments of God.
6. Again, Beza is emphasizing the simplicity of God. Even the attributes of God must be seen as inseparable from the essence of God.
7. In his work *De hypostica* Beza explains it this way: "Christ is not said to be a person in regard to both natures, but only in regard to the divine nature. The reason is because if His human nature is a person in and of itself, Christ would be composed of two persons. Therefore, the human nature is nothing other than nature which is sustained by the assuming deity, and the person of Christ is the same now as it was before the incarnation."
8. This comparison is also made in Calvin's *Institutes,* 2.14.1.
9. Or, "a third substance."
10. Eutychus (d. 454) was one of the major proponents of the doctrine of monophysitism. He stressed the fusion and the mingling of the divine and human in Christ, rather than the Chalcedonian formula of separation.
11. Christ did more than die a bodily death. His soul endured and exhausted the wrath of God during his "descent into hell."
12. For Calvin's interpretation of the descent into hell, cf. *Institutes,* 2.16.10.
13. It is necessary for Beza to make the distinction between the finitude of Christ's body and the infinitude of His deity in order to combat the Lutheran idea of consubstantiation. Cf. *De hypostica,* pg. 67: "Christ has a true body. Therefore it is visible, touchable, and locateable. And consequently it cannot be in the many various places where the Table is administered, for if it is really there, then it could be seen, touched, and sensed."
14. "Id quod dialecti Proprium quarto modo . . ."
15. By "abstract" Beza means the Godhead and humanity of Christ considered separately, as opposed to "concretely," or "as a unit."
16. Apparently Beza is not a traducianist, but a creationist. See also A105.
17. Christ is a "mean," as Beza explains later, in that He is both God and man. He is "mediator" in that He intercedes for us.
18. Again, Beza is saying the fact that Christ is mean must be understood in the context of the communication of idioms.
19. Beza is demonstrating how interrelated are all parts of systematic theology. To answer this question Beza drew upon his from discussions of the essence of God and the communication of idioms.
20. At the Council of Trent the Roman Catholic Church decided that dead saints and angels should be invoked in times of need, and that they intercede with God and Christ for us. Cf. *The Westminster Confession of Faith,* 21.3.
21. Beza says in his notes on Acts 17, "The wisdom of man is vain." Without first relying on the revelation of God man's wisdom is unable to attain to the complete truth.
22. Even in heaven the bodies of the saints are not ubiquitous.
23. In other words, when the Apostles' Creed speaks of judging the "quick and the dead," it is in reference to one's physical, not spiritual, state on the last day.
24. Traditionally, salvific or proper faith has been summed up in this way: we must acknowledge the facts (*notitia*) of God's revelation, we must assent

(*assensus*) to the truth of them, and we must trust (*fiducia*) in them. Faith rests on promises, not on wishes.

25. See A67.

26. An "accident" as used here is any property which is only incidental to a thing, and when removed, does not alter the essence of the thing. E.g., if a ball were red, and we removed the redness of the ball, it would essentially still be a ball.

27. This is often called common grace. God sustains the world for the sake of the elect.

28. That is, the "will."

29. That is, are we mere helpless machines?

30. By "spontaneously" Beza means "self-generated," or "of one's own accord."

31. Beza is reminding us that the order of salvation is logical, not temporal.

32. The analogy of faith, or *analogia fidei*, is the rule that Scripture must be interpreted by Scripture.

33. Beza is saying that we are not joined to Christ by virtue of His incarnation, but through the mysterious apprehension of Him through faith.

34. Cf. Calvin's *Institutes* 1.15 and 3.11 for Calvin's debate with Osiander. Osiander, a Lutheran theologian, taught independently that we are made righteous from Christ's divine or "essential" righteousness which He had possessed from all eternity. Instead, we are made righteous through Christ's obedience or "obtained righteousness."

35. This is called Christ's active and passive obedience.

36. The distinction that Beza is making is this: when Christ's righteousness is imputed to us we become essentially holy before God through Christ. That holiness *empowers* us to strive after our own righteousness, or a righteousness *per se*.

37. Semi-Pelagianism was revived in the 16th Century by the Jesuit theologian Luis Molina, and emphasized man's free will in obtaining his own salvation.

38. "... enim ne ex pacto ..."

39. "... minime tamen operam lusos sciamus."

40. As Luther put it, "We are saved by faith alone, but not by a faith that is alone."

41. That is, the first tablet of the Ten Commandments which speak of our duty towards God.

42. Epicurus (341-270 BC) denied the existence of the supernatural altogether, and taught that we live in a purely mechanistic material universe.

43. "*Neque enim fas est excludere a praecipui opificii mutatione decretum illud aeternum, quo paulo ante demonstravimus et omnia et singula ...*"

44. Julian the Apostate, who lived and reigned during the life of Augustine, and was a persecutor of the church.

45. Augustine's *De Civitate Dei*, 19.1.

46. This is a proverb used in both Greek and Latin Literature, meaning "No more than a river can flow up to its source." For examples, cf. Euripides, *Medea* 410 and *Propertius* 1.15-29

47. Pelagianism is the doctrine which teaches that man has the capacity within himself to take the initial steps towards salvation, even apart from the special grace of God.

48. This is in reference to a second volume of *Questions and Responses*, the contents of which are fully discussed in Raitt's work *The Eucharistic Theology of Theodore Beza.*